The SIDE EFFECT

Mark Hutchinson

ISBN: 978-1-951503-35-2

CONTENTS

1

Introduction

If you plan to drive from London to Scotland, what are the chances of there being no traffic, and of every traffic light being green throughout the whole 500-mile journey? It's unlikely, right? You will need a plan, as well as a sat-nav or a map. You are likely to hit traffic, roadblocks, diversions and multiple red lights on your way. But this won't stop you from getting to your final destination. The journey to Scotland is very much like the journey to achieving your goals. If you're running a business and need to adjust your product line, this may be your diversion. When sales are not as fast as you hoped they would be, this is potentially your traffic. Achieving goals is all about perception – realising that most things are just roadblocks and traffic, and they won't stop you from getting there in the end.

Goal setting is a process used more widely than people might think. Many of the great minds of the world and the most successful profess to goal setting and have acclaimed its impact on their lives. Most, however, will tell you to begin your goal setting journey by "writing it down" or "creating a goal board". However, in addition to this, I have found there is not much other advice on HOW to "write it down" or what process to follow. Over the course of my adult life, I have developed a strategy towards goal setting that I can wholeheartedly say has greatly impacted my success today. It is for this reason that I have written this book - to share what I have learnt.

Scenario

As you are sitting there, reading this, you may already have in mind one or more goals you want to achieve for yourself in the future. Perhaps it's your dream home, that car you have always wanted or the empire you see yourself building. Whatever it is, you have something in mind and you crave it.

To make these "dreams" become a reality, you must first turn your wants into goals, and that is exactly what will be covered within this book. There are numerous important factors in the process of goal setting, many of which you may not have considered, such as the language you use when writing them down. My aim is to help you to efficiently set your goals, track them and reflect on your progress, and so we begin.

What to expect from this book

Whether you are new to goal setting or have been setting goals for some time, as you progress through these chapters, you will find not only a number of simple steps to follow when setting your goals but also activities and exercises to help you realise which goals are the most important to you. There will also be clear and appropriate examples to make your goal setting process as efficient as possible.

My goal by the end of this book is for you to feel confident in your ability to write down your goals efficiently, a sense of empowerment from the clarity of what you truly want in life, and a sense of understanding in your capacity to train your brain for success. The aim should be to live a life of intention and purpose by figuring out your true identity and, in turn, filter out the goals that are truly important to you and build strong habits to project you towards achieving them.

Habits

Habits are the framework for success. We often feel like we need boosts of motivation which, of course, certainly help. But, overall, it is the success habits that you adopt that will ensure you are continuously and intentionally taking the steps to achieve your goals.

By the end of this book I want you to start actively introducing positive habits into your daily routine. Where most people fall short when trying to adopt positive habits is when they try to adopt too many at once. Remember: this is a marathon not a sprint.

Pick one positive habit that you would like to implement each month and build up to 12 by the end of the year.

If you stick to your new positive 'habit' for 30 days then reward yourself. It is important to celebrate your wins and they will further motivate you.

Examples of positive habits:

Wake up early	Exercise	Practice gratitude
Write daily goals (Chapter 19)	Read 30 mins per day	Visualise goals
Be consciously positive	Meditate	Manage your time

You vs Them

I have found setting goals incredibly important whilst progressing through my life. I am lucky to have had guidance when I first started out from mentors in my then profession, who were in the habit of goal setting. However, I was not given a comprehensive guide akin to the one I have created in this book.

One common mistake I have found when discussing goals with students and mentees and at talks is that most people select their goals based on what I would call "cultural surroundings'. This is the web of beliefs, habits, practices, and mythologies you have absorbed from society that tell you how you should live your life, such as the following:

- You should get that degree.
- You should work until you're sixty-five and then enjoy life.
- You should get a nine to five job.
- You should get married.
- You should have children.

These goals do not always serve your happiness; instead, they serve an ideology upheld by many cultures. This isn't your fault. You are just a product of your circumstance, but it doesn't have to be that way.

You must first be open-minded enough to be completely honest with yourself. The best way to choose goals that align with your happiness is to first ask yourself these three important questions.

22. What amazing experiences do you want to have in your life?
23. What will help you grow and become the person you want to be and the best version of yourself?
24. In what ways can you/do you want to give back?

The aim of these questions is to help you gain clarity with respect to what is most important to you by cutting through the clutter and noise and allowing you to focus on goals that will result in fulfilment and happiness. I am no stranger to striving to achieve goals that in reality I did not want to achieve, based on my surroundings and external influences. It is essential to dig deep and discover the difference between what you really want and what you "like the idea of'.

Hurdles are an extremely important factor in helping you to discover which goals are most aligned with your highest values.

Hurdles will be covered in a later chapter, but you can go as far as writing down a goal in full without realising it is something that you think you want, rather what you really want. It won't be until you come across a hurdle, a difficulty in achieving your goal, that you realise it is not really what you want. How will you know? You will either give up or carry on.

This can be very frustrating to people, as well as disappointing and disheartening, as they have spent time writing out their goals and planning for them, only to fail to achieve them. But this is the result of not spending a sufficient amount of time trying to work out what genuinely means the most to you and is most aligned with your core values.

Limiting beliefs can be critical on your journey to achieving your goals. There is a whole chapter within this book based purely on psychology and the impact of goal setting on your subconscious mind. However, if your internal monologue, the little voice in the back of your mind, is self-critical and pessimistic, then you are cheating yourself. You must start with a mindset congruent with success, because believing you can is the first step.

Over 90% of people do not write down their goals, yet doing so achieves a number of things:

- It makes you accountable
- It gives you focus
- It reinforces your commitment to your goals
- It helps you remember them
- It brings the goal psychologically closer

Not writing down your goals is like going to the supermarket without a list; it's likely you will forget something.

Bonus activity: If you'd like to verify the importance of goals, ask the most successful person you know if they have ever written down their goals. I'd be surprised if many of you received a "no" to this question.

'If you are working on something that you really care about, you don't have to be pushed. The vision pulls you.'

—Steve Jobs

2

The Psychology of Goal Setting

Language is psychologically important in the goal setting process and can have a direct impact on your motivation to achieve your goals and your mindset. Positive affirmations are one of the key ingredients for creating a positive mindset, and can influence your subconscious so that you have a more positive outlook.

For those of you learning what affirmations are for the first time, here is an insight:

Positive affirmations

Using affirmations is a way of gaining conscious control over your thoughts. Affirmations are powerful statements that, if you say them to yourself regularly, can train your mind to think more positively. Each and every thought you have is an affirmation. Each and every thing you say is an affirmation. Every time you say something negative about yourself, you are affirming that to be the truth, and this will attract negativity and further negative thoughts.

Using affirmations, you can train your brain to think in a more positive, motivational way. Affirmations serve as declarations of what you truly think of yourself and the world around you. For example: if you look at yourself in the mirror every day and pick faults in who you are, all you will ever do and all you will ever see are those faults. However, if you stand in front of the mirror and only focus on the things you like about yourself, over time you will begin to see more of the positives. Your mind will naturally create a more positive perception of yourself, and of life in general. The idea behind positive affirmations is to uplift and inspire you through the creation of self-affirming and self-empowering affirmations.

In the beginning, when you initially affirm positive thoughts and statements to yourself, they may not be true. But over time, and with repetition, they start to sink into your subconscious mind and you begin to believe them. They eventually become your reality, a self-fulfilling prophecy.

As you continue to affirm these positive statements to yourself, they will begin to overwrite any limiting or negative beliefs that you hold about yourself or your ability to achieve your goals. Your negative thoughts become positive, which in turn instils confidence, self-belief, drive, ambition, and much more.

Here are a few examples of positive affirmations for confidence:

- I am a naturally confident person
- I am confident when speaking in public
- I am confident and love meeting new people
- Confidence comes naturally to me

A shy or unconfident person could repeat these affirmations by writing them down and then saying them aloud, either to themselves or to someone else. This may initially be uncomfortable for you, especially to say aloud a statement you do not yet believe, but when you are on your own, standing in front of a mirror and getting your whole body involved (use hand movements, really act as if you believe what you are saying) this can start the process of cementing these affirmations into your mind.

Using positive affirmations gives you control over your mind and the information it receives. It puts you back in the driver's seat; you're the captain of your ship. You're in control and this helps the positive statements about who you want to be become, who you are, and how you see yourself.

Have you ever seen someone who's passionate about a topic they're speaking about? It's almost as if their whole body is communicating and it's not just them speaking the words. Think about Gary Vaynerchuk when he is addressing an audience; he captivates the room not just because of what he is saying but because his whole body expresses his passion about what he is saying. This is because he believes what he is saying with absolute certainty, whether this is true or not.

'Whether you think you can or whether you think you can't, you are both usually right.'

– Henry Ford

Here are some simple exercises that can help you start practising. The first involves writing down affirmations and the second involves your physiology

Exercise One: Start by picking an affirmation of your choice. It could be anything, but here is my example:

* I love myself and I am comfortable in my own skin.

I want you to get a journal or notepad and write this line down ten times. Put the date at the top and sign your name at the bottom of the page.

Exercise Two: Say this same phrase in the mirror ten times every morning whilst smiling. Get your hands and body involved as if you mean it – as if you want to share something with the world and speak like you want to be heard. I know this might seem slightly crazy at first, but the whole idea of this is to do something dramatic to get you out of your comfort zone. This will shock your body into taking action.

This is one of my favourite techniques which I learnt when studying the work of Anthony Robbins. This truly was a game changer for me, as it advanced me into becoming the person I am now. Not only did it increase my confidence, it also worked in many other aspects of my life. For example, I also used it for business and capital growth. 'I attract an abundance of wealth into my life' is one particular affirmation I have been using for a long time. This has kept me motivated throughout business projects and entrepreneurial ventures, instilling a belief in myself that this is what I will achieve.

When a Positive Affirmation is actually a Negative Affirmation

I want to introduce and explain a statement that may initially sound positive to you but has something to it that could be damaging.

Example: Shaun is writing down his goals and affirmations, and writes: 'I will not give up on my dreams.' This may appear to be a positive thing but let's take another look at the sentence.

I will not give up on my dreams.
I will not give up on my dreams.
I will not give up on my dreams.
I will not give up on my dreams.
I will not give up on my dreams.

Now let's look back at our initial example… I will **not** give up on my dreams.

The brain may often ignore the negative and that is exactly why this 'positive statement' can actually work against you. If I told you, "Don't think about a black cat", you would naturally start to picture a black cat… now why is that? Let me explain.

Imagine a three-year-old toddler is told, "Don't push that button." It is more than likely that they will go and push the button, regardless of the parent telling them to do the opposite.

Because the toddler's brain is ignoring the word 'not', they are hearing 'Do push that button', leaving the parents once again frustrated as to why their child will not respond to this command in the way that they want.

I will **not** give up on my dreams.
I will **not** give up on my dreams.
I will **not** give up on my dreams.
I will **not** give up on my dreams.
I will **not** give up on my dreams.

Now we can see, by looking at this affirmation in a different light, that all the brain may hear is:

I will give up on my dreams.

Let's say Shaun writes the original affirmation down as a reminder in his journal every day, five to ten times, reading it back to himself in his head and also reading it out loud. He experiences almost consistent encouragement to give up on his dreams! I found this type of psychology fascinating, as speaking to successful people made me realise that several of them already knew this secret.

I had heard about people making a 1% tweak in their life and achieving a tenfold success, such as a 1% tweak of the language that is used whilst writing affirmations. But I was curious to find out how or why, and I began questioning them about these small changes that were having significant impacts on their lives. And the more I asked, the more language was the answer.

The story of Acer and Apollo comes to mind, a story that I encountered in a previous employment position. Acer and Apollo were two racehorses that went head to head with each other in a race for the title. The first prize was £100,000 per race, with the second prize being £10,000. Of the ten races, Apollo won them all. His owners walked away with £1,000,000, whereas the horse in second place, Acer, earned only £100,000. The difference between the winner and second place for all races was a matter of half an inch: a photo finish. Yet such a small 1% difference made ten times more money!

This just goes to show that success is not always down to a crazy difference in results. It can be a small change that makes such a big difference. Something as simple as changing a few words is paramount to your success when writing out goals, but is even more important in psychologically bringing the goal closer to you.

Let's re-arrange that earlier sentence into something more positive than the negative self-sabotage affirmation.

I persist until I succeed.

So now we have the psychology under way; we can begin looking further at the process.

'The pessimist sees difficulty in every opportunity, the optimist sees the opportunity in every difficulty.'

—Winston Churchill

3

Recognising the truth

Not everyone will support you

One thing I had to understand very early on is that not everyone will support you, even if they think your business idea or goal is amazing. I personally spent way too much time questioning why my friends and family were not supporting me and buying my product or promoting it to other people. At first you may take it personally, I certainly did, and that's okay. But you need to realise that it's not because your family/friends are horrible people; a big part of their reaction is that they would love to do what you're doing but feel they can't take the sort of risks you are taking.

It's important to remember that they don't hate you or your idea, they may be dissatisfied with themselves as you may be seen as a reminder of their lack of "success". The biggest tip I can give you is to keep friends and business as separate as possible; rely only on yourself and keep pushing – you have nothing to prove to anyone but yourself.

You will be sacrificing something else

When you first start goal setting, it is very easy to think that everything can be achieved now that you have written it down; however, writing the goal down isn't enough. Continuing your current lifestyle will not help you on your path to achieving your goals. Your level of "free time" will likely, although probably not permanently, be a thing of the past as you will need to sacrifice in order to succeed.

Your goals will need time allocated to them, and the bigger the goal, the more time that will be required. You will need time to work on your goals, they won't work on themselves. I personally have had to sacrifice time with family and friends, and work through the night in order to achieve goals, because without hard work it will be difficult to get anywhere. Goal setting is simply the tool to help you focus and empower yourself to work on the goals; the hard work and motivation have to come from you.

Achieving goals is not easy, but it has been scientifically demonstrated that, as humans, we feel a deeper level of fulfilment when achieving goals after we have made sacrifices to get there.

> *'Nothing in the world is worth having or worth doing unless it means effort, pain, difficulty... I have never in my life envied a human being who led an easy life. I have envied a great many people who led difficult lives and led them well.'*
>
> *— Theodore Roosevelt*

S.M.A.R.T Goals

An extremely common "research result" when beginning goal setting is that of 'S.M.A.R.T. Goals'. Although this is a recognised method of setting goals, in my opinion it can be detrimental to your growth depending on how you view the steps. Although many would disagree with this statement, significant research into this claim has been conducted and, through this, Forbes Magazine has argued that one step in particular can be psychologically damaging when setting goals, as explained below:

The idea underlying this technique is that the goals need to be S.M.A.R.T.

- Specific
- Measurable
- Attainable
- Realistic
- Time bound

This is the common phrase you'll hear when setting goals and I agree with all but one to a certain degree.

Realistic: From my days as a broker in the city, I quickly learnt that the word itself is one of the most self-sabotaging terms you can use and can lead to notably limiting beliefs. To have this as one of your values in achieving serious goals can leave you with nothing but frustration.

Stop and think about that word for a minute and ask yourself: 'Who do you know, whether they be in the public eye or not, who has achieved something great and initially thought it was unrealistic?' If they had thought this, they would never have started.

The concept of realistic is subjective; each person will have a different idea as to what they can realistically achieve. However, the word realistic could limit your belief in yourself. Elon Musk may have had people tell him it was unrealistic to start an electric car brand that would make people look at the motoring industry in a completely different way. However, he saw it as within his capability. He may not have known he would get as far as he has with Tesla but he knew that, in reality, almost nothing is unrealistic.

In the 1950s, most people believed that it was impossible to run a mile in under four minutes. One man did not; his name was Roger Banister. In 1954, Roger Banister broke the four-minute barrier with a world record time of three minutes fifty-nine seconds. He had achieved a goal that nobody thought was possible. After Roger had broken the four-minute barrier, a strange thing happened. People began setting goals to run a mile in under four minutes and were succeeding, whereas previously they had tried and failed. In the three years after Roger Banister ran a mile in under four minutes, sixteen other runners had done the same thing. So my question to you is: what is your psychological barrier? What is your 'four-minute mile'? What is keeping you from breaking through it?

The point I am trying to get across is to take care not to let the limiting beliefs of others affect the goals you set, because what you can achieve is up to you, not those around you. What is stopping you from reaching your goals? If it is limiting beliefs, then you are talking yourself out of success.

Don't get confused: if your goal within the next two weeks is to be a millionaire with no business up and running or no solid plan, then of course that is likely to be delusional – but in terms of the language we want to use, I would personally steer away from the word realistic as it only limits your way of thinking.

The idea of realistic is something that has been imposed on each and every person by society, which then impacts your subjective way of viewing life – although to some extent 'realistic' does need to be considered, because a goal that is almost a fantasy can lead to demotivation and frustration if it is not achievable.

You should push yourself beyond your current realms of belief as you can do more than you currently imagine, but not so far that you end up in another dimension.

If you want realistic results, you will do something realistic. If you want good results, you will do something that is good. If you want great results, you will do something great. If you want to totally dominate the industry you are in, then your way of thinking to the majority of people will be totally unrealistic. If you share these kinds of ideas with people and they have a differing viewpoint, then you are most likely on the right path.

'Impossible is just a big word thrown around by small men who find it easier to live in the world they've been given than to explore the power they have to change it. Impossible is not a fact. It's an opinion. Impossible is not a declaration. It's a dare. Impossible is potential. Impossible is temporary. Impossible is nothing.'

—Muhammad Ali

4

Define your Vision – The Future You

Before setting out to achieve any goals, it is important that you first establish a clear vision of what your ideal life would be like. At this stage, it is not about making it 'perfect'. This is going to be your first draft and, as you go through the steps outlined, you may even find that goals you thought were important are no longer as important as you believed.

Having a clear vision is what will keep you moving forward to overcome the hurdles you may face. This is where some people can get confused when they lack motivation as, a lot of the time, it has nothing to do with their drive to achieve goals and more to do with the lack of clarity of their vision.

This is why spending a significant amount of time being as clear as possible about what you truly want is worth its weight in gold.

How to start

'All successful people are big dreamers. They imagine what their future could be, ideal in every respect, and then they work every day toward their distant vision, that goal or purpose.' Brian Tracy

Start off by imagining how you see your ideal life, 'The Future You'. Imagine you have achieved the goals you are setting out to achieve. What does your future you look like? What have you achieved?

How has your life changed in each of these key areas?

Income - How much do you want to earn this year, next year and many years from today?

Think about what types of income you would like to create. Is this income a skill set you possess? Or maybe even 'passive' income? It may even be a future business you are looking to create. It's important to start to draft out what this looks like in the future.

Family and Relationships - What kind of lifestyle do you want to create for yourself and your family?

Think about how you see your relationships with your family, and even your friends. What would be ideal in this scenario? Think about your future relationships with your significant other. Do you want to have children? And what would that look like to you?

Health - How would your health be different if you could have it the way you wanted it?

Imagine your ideal physical (and mental) shape. What does that look like? How do you see yourself and how do others see you? And how will that change in the future?

Net Worth - How much do you want to accumulate in your working/entrepreneurial life?

It's important to not be attached to particular numbers but, at the same time, it's also important that we strive towards something. Is there a specific portfolio of assets that you would like to own prior to retirement? How do you want to set yourself up for the longer term, and maybe even leave a legacy?

Personal Development - What kind of person are you? How do others see you?

In life, personal growth never ends. We are always growing and learning new things. As you grow as an individual, you become a different person, in any unit of time. Really start to think about what areas you want to develop. This can range from the books you want to read and the courses you want to take to tapping into a more spiritual side. All in all, it is absolutely necessary to go into as much detail as possible about how you envisage this, whilst remaining aware that it is likely to change as you continue to grow.

Exercise: Consider the goals you are setting yourself now, the ones you have just imagined achieving, and split them into short-term, medium-term and long-term goals. Now write yourself a letter in which you explain all of the above, what goals you achieved to get to your future self, what you had to do to achieve them, and how it feels now that you are there. Go as far as describing your daily routine, include all the details you can think of. What would your morning routine look like and consist of? Would it include reading, exercise, meditation? Get down to the essential details of exactly how you envision this.

It is important to be clear about what success means to you.

Identity

Now you have visualised and become clear on the future vision of your life it is time to start thinking about your identity.

The current 'identify' you hold for yourself may not be serving you and you may not be happy with it. You will reaffirm your identity to yourself on a daily basis so you need to ensure your future identity is congruent with your future vision and where you want to go in life.

Your identity should act as a pillar for making good decisions. If your identity is unclear then making important choices in life could seem, somewhat, challenging. However, when there is a strong sense of identity, of knowing who you are and how you would normally behave, making important life decisions becomes an easier task. Assuming everything that you have mapped out for your 'ideal vision' will go smoothly is unrealistic. This is why it is important to have a strong identity, as leaning on it will keep your focussed and on track.

My identity is: "*I am a powerful creator of my future.*" Think about what your identity is and how this correlates to your ideal vision. Your identity may not come to you straight away, but ensure to keep this in the back of your mind as it may come to you as you progress through this book and gain more clarity on the bigger picture.

'The way to get started is to quit talking and begin doing.'

—Walt Disney

5

---

10 Things I Want to Be, Do and Have

When people think about setting goals, it is extremely common to focus mainly on the materialistic: for example, a specific car they want to own, or perhaps an expensive watch. This is natural, a default, but what you need to do and what you need to be should also be considered in order to achieve some materialistic goals. There are also goals that are just solely 'do' or 'be' that many people, and likely you as you are reading this book, also want to achieve.

In this section, the aim for you is to dig as deeply into your subconscious as you can to become clear about what you truly want. Through experience I have found that a good way to filter this out is to first list 10 things you want to do, be and have.

For example:

Be   -   To be confident at public speaking
Do   -   To climb a mountain
Have -   To have a red Ferrari

You'll come up with 30 goals in total for the next 12 months/10 years, whatever time scale you set for yourself (short, medium or long term), that you will focus on achieving.

When you begin, the ideas may initially flow very quickly. But as you get closer and closer to having ten of each, you may struggle to fill each column. You may also write down ten and then realise there are other goals you have not included that mean more to you. Remember: at this stage you are still on your first draft and it is okay to adjust what you have. The best way to counter this is to ignore the number first, ignore 10. Just write three lists of everything you want to do, be and have over the next twelve months. This may take some time to complete, perhaps a number of days or even a week of continuing to return to it, but when you have complete lists, review those that have more than 10 and filter out any goals you are not initially drawn to. These will usually be goals you feel you should achieve but do not actually have the urge to do so.

Be

When you sit and think about yourself as a whole, not just your physical appearance but your personality, all aspects of your being, what would you say you could most improve on? What would you most like to improve on? That is what this set of 10 things is about. If you were to imagine yourself in 12 months' time, who would you want to be?

Do

One of the biggest reasons why a person would set a 'do' goal would be to feel fulfilled. Money is not likely to be a big enough incentive and 'doing goals' can help you to develop and grow as a person. I feel this is where the saying "money doesn't buy you happiness" correlates as, although material possessions may be easy for you to obtain, if you feel you are not doing anything fulfilling in your life then you could be left feeling empty and unsatisfied. The novelty of material possessions can wear off very quickly, but you cannot buy back the time to do things.

Have

These are your material desires. They are natural and perfectly okay. They are your passions and the rewards for your hard work.

Do

1. _____

_____

2. _____

_____

3. _____

_____

4 _____

_____

5. _____

_____

6. _____

_____

7. _____

_____

8. _____

_____

9. _____

_____

10._____

_____

Be

1. _____

_____

2. _____

_____

3. _____

_____

4 _____

_____

5. _____

_____

6. _____

_____

7. _____

_____

8. _____

_____

9. _____

_____

10._____

_____

Have

1. _____

_____

2. _____

_____

3. _____

_____

4 _____

_____

5. _____

_____

6. _____

_____

7. _____

_____

8. _____

_____

9. _____

_____

10._____

_____

Now that you have your initial thirty goals, narrow them down to the 9 (3 of each) that you feel are the most important. Although the other 21 are still goals you are going to aim to achieve and would like to achieve in your allotted timeline, these 9 goals are the most important to you and therefore are those you will be the most motivated to achieve.

Be

1. _____

_____

2. _____

_____

3. _____

_____

Do

1. _____

_____

2. _____

_____

3. _____

_____

Have

1. _____

_____

2. _____

_____

3. _____

_____

'The ultimate reason for setting goals
is to entice you to become the person it
takes to achieve them.'

—Jim Rohn

6

Set a Date

Deadlines

Deadlines can be crucial when goal setting because, with a timeframe, your subconscious brain is unlikely to motivate you to push yourself to achieve the goal due to there being no allotted timescale. Have you ever been given a deadline at work? You work harder to meet the deadline as you don't want to miss it. Your unconscious mind will do the self-same thing when goal setting. Imagine it is a little person on your shoulder, constantly reminding you to do something. He or she will continuously remind you to work on your goals and keep you on track without even realising.

I myself have noticed this when goal setting. I often set my '10 things I want to be, do and have' goals a year in advance and forget that I have written some of them down as there were so many and some were particularly small. When revisiting these goals months later, I realised I have achieved them without consciously putting effort into it. This is because my unconscious mind has kept me on track and pushed me to work towards a goal and make it happen without me even being aware of it. The power of your unconscious brain is amazing as it is often not until you review your goals that you see how far you have come. If for some reason you don't achieve your goal by the deadline, simply set a new deadline.

There are no unreasonable goals, only unreasonable deadlines. It is important not to become too attached to the deadline you have set yourself. Not everything will happen on your time and according to your schedule, but you will be significantly closer to your goal than if you hadn't set a date at all.

Exercise Four: The Theory of Constraints – There is always at least one limiting factor or constraint that sets the speed at which you achieve your goal; what is it for you? For each of the nine goals you have written down, write down a deadline by which you would like to achieve these goals and state what the biggest constraint is, whether it is seeing things through, being consistent, etc.

An example of this could be:

Goal - To become 10% body fat with lean muscle
Deadline - On or before 31.12.2021
Constraints - Temptation of fast food, cravings, procrastination

1. Goal _____

_____

Deadline _____

Constraint _____

2. Goal _____

_____

Deadline _____

Constraint _____

3. Goal _____

_____

Deadline _____

Constraint _____

4. Goal _____

_____

Deadline _____

Constraint _____

5. Goal _____

_____

Deadline _____

Constraint _____

6. Goal _____

_____

Deadline _____

Constraint _____

7. Goal _____

_____

Deadline _____

Constraint _____

8. Goal _____

_____

Deadline _____

Constraint _____

9. Goal _____

_____

Deadline _____

Constraint _____

10. Goal _____

_____

Deadline _____

Constraint _____

It is important, however, to understand that we cannot plan for every potential constraint. This is where we can apply the art of releasing control.

Releasing control is when you set a date, for whatever goal you are focusing on, but, at the same time, you release control of trying to predict every single situation that you may need to mitigate along the way. Life can throw curve balls so it's important to not put too much pressure on yourself to have predicted every single one of them.

The 80/20 Rule

The 80/20 rule is the idea that 80% of the reasons for not achieving your goals come from within yourself, only 20% are external.

The 80% that relates to you may be a lack of motivation, a tendency to be a procrastinator, a lack of skills, or not having the necessary knowledge required, to name but a few examples. The 20% that relates to external factors tends to be your 'excuses' and is usually something beyond your control, long working days for example. This immediately demonstrates the need to work on yourself as it is more important to begin by considering how you can improve your chances before you start worrying about external matters.

I don't want you to rely on these excuses, and in the majority of cases you will be able to overcome them. Obviously, if you are working sixteen-hour days, then going to the gym may be difficult, but there is always time to prioritise the things that mean the most to you, aligning your priorities with your goals. In this case, those who work from nine to five may use the excuse that they have little time to go to the gym, along with their other daily pressures such as housework, travel cooking, etc. However, a one-hour workout is only 4.16% of your day. When you put your 'excuse' into perspective, there is usually little reason for this excuse. This method can be used to counteract the majority of external constraints, as they are often easy to overcome.

However, to use the above mentioned example again, if for one day or one week you are required to work overtime which means you cannot get to the gym, don't allow yourself to become frustrated. This is not a case of being unable to achieve your goals; it is just an external factor that is a slight constraint. It's important to know it's okay if you're not 100% motivated every single day. Although there will be days that take you off track, you need to start each day fresh and rebalanced so you will always be moving towards your goals.

'A dream written down with a date becomes a goal.'

—Greg S. Reid

7

Detail is Key

Write it out in specific and precise detail

When writing out your goals, it is especially important to do so in as much detail as you can think of in order to focus your mind on what you really want, using the present tense – communicating to your subconscious that the goal has achieved, as if it has already happened.

Example: A bad way of setting your goal

Goal: I want a Porsche by the end of next year. I want to save 10% of my wages every month to have a deposit for it.

Example: A good way of setting your goal

Goal: I own my Porsche 911 GT3 RS on or before 31st December 2021. It has 500 horsepower at 8250 rpm and a top speed of 193 mph. It does 0-60 in 3.1 seconds and its fuel consumption in the city is 14 mpg. The colour of my Porsche is Lava Orange with black/lava orange leather interior and lava orange seat belts. It has comfortable full bucket seats and auto-dimming mirrors with integrated rain sensors. It has heated seats and air conditioning with painted air vent slats to match the rest of the car. It has a Porsche doppelkupplung transmission which includes a 7-speed dual-clutch gearbox and a PDK SPORT button so I can drive in either automatic mode or use manual shift controls. My Porsche has 9.5J x 20inch GT3 RS platinum wheels on the front and 12.5J x 21inch GT3 RS platinum wheels on the back. Its base price is $175,900.

The difference between these two statements is clearly obvious.

To think about it logically, when you order a takeaway, you would not just ask for a pizza. You would ask for, for example, a mozzarella pizza with a tomato and garlic base, chestnut mushrooms, green peppers and red onions, with a cheese-stuffed crust. The same goes for a car or for any given goal. You should make it as specific as possible so that you work towards achieving exactly what you want.

Here's a worksheet to help you focus when writing down your goals, combining the first two steps.

Note: It is important to sign your name on your goals so that you feel committed to them; like signing a contract, you are committing to your goals in the same way.

Date: _____

Detailed goal description

Goal: _____

_____

_____

_____

_____

_____

_____

_____

_____

_____

_____

_____

_____

_____

Signature: _____

'I always wanted to be somebody, but now I realise I should have been more specific.'

—Lily Tomlin

8

Manageable Steps

How you structure you goals when goal setting can be important to your projected success at achieving them. If you set yourself a very large goal, such as self-building your new home, then this can feel very daunting without first breaking it down into small steps; for instance, get an architect to draw up plans, submit these to the council, get quotes from subcontractors, and so on.

A great way to start is with small steps. If we have a goal that requires a big step, it can be intimidating and can make us procrastinate regarding the tasks at hand. What we tend not to realise is that, by taking just small steps each day/week and in this way breaking the process down, we can make serious progress towards our goals.

This step gets the ball rolling and helps you to see the light at the end of the tunnel – and that reaching it is possible. Let's take an example: say your goal is to own a Lamborghini.

The small steps for this big goal may be as follows:

- Call a dealer to find the exact price of the car/deposit needed and what the monthly payments will be.

- Work out how you can offset the payments by offering a service of some kind. For example, if it's £2,000 a month for the car and you can do some affiliate marketing that makes you £2,000 a month, you are offsetting the car payments.
- Work out how much it will cost per year.
- Work out how much it will cost to run per month with fuel, insurance and road tax.

Ticking off these small steps then allows you to calculate other steps going forward, such as:

- How much do I need to make/save to offset the additional costs of owning this car without impacting my current lifestyle?
- How much longer will it take using my current rate of income and savings to pay for the deposit? (This will then allow you to set a more accurate date.)

It is likely that to achieve this goal you're going to need to push yourself out of your comfort zone. Therefore, breaking it down into smaller, more manageable, steps can make it feel more controllable.

Daily small step: write down five goals to achieve that day that will push you closer towards the long-term goal; for instance, 'I will close a deal to earn myself £500 commission.'

Weekly small step: spend two hours on an affiliate marketing scheme to generate £2,000 per month to offset the monthly payments.

Monthly small step: transfer £1,000 a month of your current earnings into a separate account that is allocated to the deposit of £20,000 for the car.

You can now see how this slowly but surely pushes you towards achieving this goal, just by having a step-by-step plan. This may seem simple, yet millions of people don't do it. It's just as easy to do as it is not to do. This is why less than 10% of people continuously and habitually set goals and push themselves to achieve them.

Even within this 10%, not all will write their goals down, which is why many of these people will not achieve the goals they initially set. There are those who are slightly more ambitious with a clearer vision of where they want to go, but without a set plan and a hard copy of their goal, more often than not they will not achieve it.

There needs to be an equilibrium between breaking down the steps too far or not enough; as both have positives and negatives. Breaking down your goals into loads of small steps is good because you have a clear idea of exactly how you will get there – but it can be demotivating if you break it down too much, as you may not meet every step exactly on time.

Larger and fewer steps can be more motivating as you have longer to achieve them, which can make them seem more attainable; however, this can cause you to lose focus on exactly how to get there.

So a happy medium is needed: a good balance. The way I found a good balance was to set daily goals but keep them small – something I will go over in the 'Daily Goals' chapter later in the book.

Goal: _____

_____

Manageable steps:

1 _____

_____

2 _____

_____

3 _____

_____

4 _____

_____

5 _____

_____

6 _____

_____

7 _____

_____

8 _____

_____

'Life is a series of steps. Things are done gradually. Once in a while there is a giant step. But most of the time we are taking small, insignificant steps on the stairway of life.'

—Ralph Ransom

9

Identify the Skills and Knowledge Required

One of the main pitfalls people encounter when goal setting is that they get so focused on having or wanting a goal that they forget that to achieve it, they may have to learn something, or even become a different person.

The first thing to do is identify who your mentors are. Who are the people you can look up to – maybe even speak to, if you are lucky enough – and who can bring you closer to achieving your goal? For example, if you want to be a successful businessman, one of your mentors/role models may be Elon Musk. To be like him, and to help you to become as successful as him, you would need to look at the skills he holds that either you don't have or you need to work on to help propel you towards your goals. A mentor could also be someone that you know: a college or university tutor, a successful member of your family, or maybe a friend.

Next, you would need to look at what specific skill(s) you require in order to achieve your goal. If you want to learn to play the guitar, a skill you require would be to read music. Although the ability to play the guitar is a skill in itself, other skills can impact on the learning process and a lack of these can hinder you on your path to reaching your goal.

You need to be specific when identifying the skills required. If you want to design your own brand, you can't just say, 'I need to be more creative.' GET SPECIFIC! For this example you may want to consider a course in illustration to learn how to do this.

At this stage, you will also need to identify the knowledge you will need to be able to achieve your goal. For example, when starting a business, you would need (at least to begin with) a basic knowledge of business. Therefore, the best way to begin to acquire this knowledge, if you don't already have it, would be to buy and read a book on how to set up a business. This may seem simple, but this is how great goals are achieved. First, you need to ask yourself what simple, specific, basic skills and knowledge you require to get you there. One small step at a time.

Once these skills and knowledge have been identified, you need to write out in small steps how you will get there. If there is certain knowledge you need to obtain, is it freely available or do you need to get it from someone in particular? In such cases, the first step you write down would be 'Meet Mr Bremner for a coffee meeting and discuss the marketing behind a new brand.' It is important to acknowledge whether specific knowledge is needed from a particular person to achieve your goal; therefore, when writing out these steps you must be specific, even to the point of using that person's name. The reason for this is because it forces you to ask yourself more relevant questions about how you will get there. You will soon realise that it is in the questions you ask yourself that you find great success.

Example: Shaun has already set a date, described his goal in detail, and been specific in the goals that he wants to achieve. He has written out manageable steps to set him on the path to starting his own business and is now identifying the skills and knowledge required to get him there.

First, he recognises that he has someone within his family – his uncle – whom he can look up to as a mentor, because the uncle is already successful in the line of business that Shaun is entering. He then looks at the difference in skills and knowledge between himself and his uncle to identify the information he will need to successfully enter this field. He should ask his uncle how he came about this knowledge and skill set and how he too can acquire this.

Shaun would write this information out separately in note form until the information is ready to be written out using the steps.

Mentor – Uncle Chris

Knowledge – ask him the following questions:

1. What are the top five books you have read that moved you closer to the position of success you are in today?
2. Is there a specific book out of these five that was a game changer for you?
3. What supplier did you use to create your product, and can they facilitate my order?

Skills – ask him the following questions:

1. What are the top five skills you would say are most important in this industry?
2. Was it through experience that you developed these or are there any particular courses or exercises I can take to improve?
3. What is the most valuable skill you have that I can learn?

Can you see what's happening here? Shaun is focusing on the specific knowledge and skills he needs to do well in the industry he is entering. He is using his uncle to identify the skills and knowledge he himself doesn't hold in order to become a success. Through this process, he is cutting down on the time that he could waste on researching the skills and knowledge needed by gaining vital first-hand knowledge from someone who has made himself a success.

If his mentor is someone of whom it is not possible to ask these questions, Shaun would have to ask himself something like the following:

Mentor: Elon Musk

Knowledge:

1. What top five books has Musk publicly recommended as helping him on his path to success?
2. What one book has been publicised as his most highly recommended book?
3. What vital pieces of knowledge can be found within these books that I don't already have?

Skills:

1. What are the skills Musk has for which he is most recognised in business?
2. In interviews he has given, has he suggested whether these skills were gained through experience or has he recommended particular ways to improve on these skills?
3. What does he consider to be his most valuable skill?

Now that Shaun has the answers to these questions, he can write them down with his goal as follows:

Example: Knowledge and Skills

I am reading 'The Chimp Paradox' by Dr Steve Peters to gain the knowledge required to control my emotions within difficult business situations. This is going to ensure that I build good customer and supplier relations and move closer towards my goal of becoming successful in this field. I look up to both my uncle and Dr S Peters as mentors, as they both possess this knowledge.

I have enrolled in a course on illustration that I attend once a week as it fits comfortably around work. This is going to help me build the skills required to design my products, which will move me closer towards my goal of being a fulltime business owner.

I have given one example each of the skills and knowledge Shaun could detail whilst writing out his goals. I must stress that there will be more than one skill and one section of knowledge needed to achieve your goals, and I urge you to be as specific and in-depth as possible within this section.

As you can see, this section not only helps you start to acknowledge the skills and knowledge required, it also prompts you to take action.

Possible Mentors:

1. _____ 2. _____

3. _____ 4. _____

Knowledge questions to ask:

1. _____

_____

2. _____

_____

3. _____

_____

Skills questions to ask:

1. _____

_____

2. _____

_____

3. _____

_____

Knowledge and Skills:

1. _____

_____

_____

2. _____

_____

_____

3. _____

_____

_____

4. _____

_____

_____

5. _____

_____

_____

6. _____

_____

_____

7. _____

_____

_____

8. _____

_____

_____

9. _____

_____

_____

'Know first who you are, and then adorn
yourself accordingly.'

—Epictetus

10

Identify Your Obstacles

This is one of my favourite sections. The majority of the time the things you perceive to be obstacles are, in fact, not obstacles at all. The obstacles that may spring to mind when you first think of them are things like time, money, contacts, etc. However, the only real obstacle is yourself. When you realise that it is only you getting in the way of your goals and dreams, you can begin to make what you want happen.

Taking responsibility is key because when you accept that it's you, and only you, holding yourself back, your mind begins to dig deep into your subconscious to adjust old patterns of thought and create new ones. Accepting responsibility triggers you to start asking empowering questions. When you develop this type of attitude, you will always find your way around an obstacle. No matter what it is, that inner voice of yours will condition itself to think of another way round it. If you get stuck, do you just give up? Or do you pivot and accept it for what it is and move on? This is easier said than done and, granted, it took me a while to become good at this. Pivoting is a skill, as it is so very easy to get caught up in your business idea; for example, you limit yourself by thinking your initial route is the only one. If you hit a road-block, be open-minded enough to take a different route.

I like to consider the other things that stand in the way of achieving your goals as 'minor hurdles'. Instead of viewing them as an 'obstacle' that is blocking your way, view them as a hurdle; the word in itself makes the task seem easier to overcome, as we leap forward.

Now let's start with three examples of possible hurdles.

- Parents – Instinctively, most parents will want to protect their children so don't take it personally if they are not 100% supportive of your ideas at first. Now this isn't one of the moments that you start thinking of your parents as a true obstacle and start resenting them; see them instead as a minor hurdle, because they want, they think, the best for you. If your parents are not that supportive of you being an entrepreneur, then I'm not surprised as it's seen as 'risky'. Keeping your goals to yourself can sometimes be a good thing as, nine times out of ten, once you have a solid plan and your parents see how serious you are, they will support you.

Example: Shaun is young and ambitious with a hunger for business. His parents care about him, so naturally want him to strive for a higher education and get good grades. Although they think his business plan is a good idea, they do not want him to leave school at sixteen to pursue a business instead of going to college and onto university.

- Friends – This again may seem a strange choice but your friends can appear to be a hurdle on your way towards your goals. They can potentially hold you back. Accept this, don't question it, and move on. If they do not support you, it will often be a reflection of their own insecurities rather than your own.

Example: Shaun is very fitness- and health-orientated. He likes to work out and eat healthy food in order to maintain his body and keep it in good shape. However, Shaun's friends do not share this interest. They enjoy eating at fast food restaurants before going out on a Saturday night to drink. This is often Shaun's only chance to see his friends due to separate work and other commitments. Therefore, Shaun may often go along on these nights with his friends, which will impact on his fitness goal as his friends have no interest in many of the social activities he enjoys.

- Capital – This may seem like a difficult hurdle to overcome because, with money, it's either there or it isn't. However, if you think of it like this, you will find it difficult to overcome. This brings me onto empowering questions that will help you overcome hurdles such as this.

Empowering Questions

Generally, as humans, we focus on the negative. I am sure we've all fallen into that trap of 'when it rains, it pours.' What about changing that thought process by managing your 'inner narrator'? What if, when it rains, it just rains? This comes in the form of acceptance, which is something you're going to want to hold as a value; while accepting that goals may take time, you can still be incredibly successful in reaching them.

A change of language can make all the difference. Make a conscious effort to understand how you speak to yourself and ask yourself questions that are going to empower you and bring you closer to your goals rather than push you further away. I honestly believe that within each of us is a hidden genius; sometimes we just need some help to unlock it. Asking yourself empowering questions not only helps you to think positively, it gets you asking the right questions and, in turn, enables you to find the desired answer.

Ask something one way and you'll end up with limiting beliefs, thoughts that resemble the stereotypical 'I'm never going to be able to buy that'. Ask it another way and you'll find yourself having thoughts like 'What books are successful people reading right now on how to achieve multiple sources of income?' This is how you tap into new thought patterns. My idea and rationale behind this is that, deep down, we already know what we need to do – we just have to start asking the right questions. I want you all to remember: 'it only costs zero pounds to think like a millionaire.'

Asking empowering questions is key, as it focuses your mind on thinking about the means of reaching your goal. It gets you asking the right questions, thus pushing you towards your goals much faster.

Instead of asking 'how will I afford to buy that Ferrari?' you need to ask yourself 'how can I triple my income, along with providing a product or service that will add value to someone, in order to be able to buy my Ferrari?'

Instead of asking 'how will I ever do that?' ask yourself 'what skill(s) do I want to become really good at? What can I do today to start to master them?'

Let's say you want to learn to play the guitar. The best way to ask yourself how to achieve this would be to structure it in this way: 'What video on YouTube can I watch today in order to start learning to play the guitar? Where can I find a good guitar teacher?'

You are your only obstacle.

Here are the seven most common paths that can lead to self-sabotage:

1. Trying to do too much – The reason behind the 10 things I want to do, be and have and then narrowing it down to 3 of each, is to focus your mind on what you really want. When you have your top nine, your aim should be to actively focus on these. If you were actively trying to achieve all 30 at once your mind would likely become so overwhelmed and stretched between them all that you will not have enough time to focus on them and take sufficiently big steps towards reaching them. This could lead to you becoming demotivated, procrastinating and ultimately

giving up. Have you ever been in a situation where you have so much to do that you end up doing nothing at all? This isn't to say that you can't be driven and set lots of goals, but there needs to be a balance.

2. Remaining in your comfort zone – It is human nature to remain in a position where you feel comfortable and safe. Have you ever stayed in a job for longer than you know you should just because you knew what was expected of you and it had become almost second nature? When you moved out from your parents' house(s), did it take you longer than you had initially planned, and did you do it later in life than you had originally thought you would? This is because when we are in a known environment it feels safer and therefore we find it difficult to stretch the boundaries and break the mould because we become complacent.

3. Being stuck in the past – If you continue to dwell on the past, on what you could have done differently and/or better, you may miss the opportunity to make the change today to live a better tomorrow. If you allow the past to consume you, then today will eventually become tomorrow/next week/next month/next year, and you will waste your life on 'shoulda, coulda, woulda's'. It's important to be aware of this so as not to continue like a broken record.

4. Not taking consistent action and procrastinating – Have you ever said to yourself 'Oh, I have ages to do that, I can do it tomorrow'? Procrastination and inconsistently working on your goals is a major hindrance to reaching them. You can find yourself forever living on 'Tomorrow Island', where everything is always pushed back a day but in reality never gets done. By setting daily goals, which you will read about more in a later chapter in this book, you can keep your mind focused and continually work on your goals on a daily basis.

5. Fear – The fear of the unknown and the fear of taking risks can stop you working towards your goals altogether. It makes you feel uncomfortable; therefore, to overcome

this, you need to discover the source of the fear. What is it that you are really afraid of? Fear can convince you to stay where you are in case you fail and can cripple you when attempting to achieve your goals. Fear is just False Evidence Appearing Real. You have two options: Let fear force you into walking away from your goals, or take a bold stand against fear and let it serve you, fuel you, and drive you on.

6. Pessimistic voices – The analogy of the devil and angel on your shoulders comes to mind. The devil will attempt to poison your mind and will show you all the reasons why you cannot reach your goal. As humans, we are psychologically programmed to remember bad events/feelings/emotions we have experienced. Therefore, we are instinctively more likely to remember all the reasons for not doing something rather than the reasons for doing it, which may in fact outweigh all the negatives.

7. You don't give a f*** – This is when you have set yourself a goal, maybe to impress others or because it is something you think you should want, that in reality you do not want at all. You think it sounds good and you like the idea of it but in reality, if it did not come about, you wouldn't care. If you find yourself telling yourself 'I just need to get motivated' then it's not as important to you as you may have first thought. This could quite simply be down to the fact that you don't hold the values required in order to achieve that goal, or you don't care enough. Quite simply, you just don't give a f***.

These are seven dreadful ingredients that lead to a cocktail of disaster, leaving a very sour taste in your mouth. If you're sitting there thinking that this is you and you are unsure what to do, this is easily and simply combatted, and I'll show you how. Daily goals, values and affirmations (Chapter 19) will help you tackle this cocktail of negativity and will lead you to overcoming your main obstacle – yourself.

As well as the daily goals method, when writing out your obstacles and hurdles in full you should positively word the solutions.

Example: Shaun has issues speaking to his parents about his goals and ambitions. This is because they feel the best thing for him would be to continue within education for as long as possible rather than leaving school at sixteen to start a business, thus taking a big risk. It is important for him to be aware that his parents are only doing this because they care, even though their wish may not be the best thing for him. Therefore, he recognises this as a hurdle on the path to achieving his goal.

He WOULD NOT write: 'My parents are a hurdle as I cannot discuss my dreams with them', as this brings negativity into his goal setting, which could have a detrimental effect.

He WOULD write: 'I am focusing on discussing my ideas with likeminded individuals who can give me subjective and unbiased feedback that will continue to push me towards my goals'.

Ultimately, after reviewing what we have discussed above, it becomes clear that what we think stands in your way are minor hurdles and, in reality, the only obstacle to achieving your goal is you and the excuses you tell yourself on a daily basis.

Exercise: Identify the biggest five hurdles standing in your way of achieving your goal and address them with a solution.

1. Hurdle _____

Solution _____

2. Hurdle _____

Solution _____

3. Hurdle _____

Solution _____

4. Hurdle _____

Solution _____

5. Hurdle _____

Solution _____

'When obstacles arise, you change your direction to reach your goal; you do not change your decision to get there.'

—Zig Ziglar

11

People to Associate With

If you read this section and start getting angry, I ask you to read the whole chapter as there is a lot to take from it. It is extremely easy for me to push people's buttons in this section and to touch raw nerves, as a lot of what I'm about to say is not what many people want to hear. But it is what they need to hear. If the wrong people remain prominent in your life, there may not be room to meet new ones.

In this section I take you through the importance of surrounding yourself with likeminded people who have either had the same success as you, or have had the success that you desire and wish to learn from. One of the biggest mistakes we make is that we fail to realise how important our social circle is and the effect it has on our goals. I have seen and experienced first-hand the effects of 'friends' subtly bringing you down to their level. The harsh truth is that some friends, and sometimes even family, are not going to be happy for your success. The more quickly you accept that, the more quickly you can get on with the show and start focusing on bringing your goals closer.

Have you ever met a group of people and thought that they all seem to be virtual clones of each other? They have similar nicknames, speak in similar ways and think the same while holding very similar views on life. This may start to sound familiar. What happens now if you are a member of that group but start to develop different thought patterns? You become more curious about goals, building businesses and income creation. It is highly likely that when you share your views, your friends will impose their common views and beliefs regarding what they think you can and can't achieve. This is because they see you as similar to themselves and cannot see themselves reaching these goals. Now here is the crazy part… you listen to them.

If you were to spend time around Elon Musk every day for a week, how do think you'd feel about what is possible in life? You'd be embarrassed to say 'I think this can't be done' etc. Why? Because you know he would laugh, as he thinks in a way that makes almost everything possible. Now we do not all have the luxury of being around such great minds like Musk, but we do have choices about who we associate with. A choice about who we spend our time and energy on. Unfortunately, your friends will not be paying your bills in the future so make sure your opinions of yourself and your capabilities are not theirs.

Who you spend time with will have a great impact on your life. If you're spending the most part of your time with people who are on a downwards spiral, have no ambition, no drive, and no interest in changing, they are likely to be dragging you down with them. 'Walk with the wise and become wise, for a companion of fools suffers harm.' – Proverbs 13:20. Whatever quality they have, good or bad, it will rub off on you.

On a lighter note, let us focus on the benefits of being around likeminded, positive people.

- Encouragement
- They push you towards your goals
- They are genuinely happy for you

- They keep you on track and pick you up when you're feeling down or stressed
- They give you honest advice rather than tell you what you want to hear
- They will support your projects

The list could go on but the key thing to take away from this is that you can spend ten years going round in circles surrounded by the wrong people, or you can surround yourself with secure, likeminded people who will push you ever closer to your goals and support you.

Here's the good news. If you associate with generous people, you'll become more generous. If you associate with successful people, you'll become successful. The same good qualities will start to rub off on you and will become a part of your life. That's why it is so important to be selective about whom you spend your time with.

Red and Green Flags

We need to consider the 'red flags' of the people we associate with and how these should deter us. We would prefer not to associate with those who are horrible to their spouses, family, kids, friends, etc; we have to set those boundaries.

Have you ever sat and listened to a friend speak about something or someone, feeling perfectly happy beforehand but after listening to their story you hold anger and resentment against the particular person or topic that has been discussed? Even though, in reality, it has no impact on you at all. Spending time with negative people impacts you in a similar way. For example, your co-worker appears to be unhappy in their relationship and so they vent their feelings to you. This starts making you think more about your own relationships; things that seemed small begin to seem larger, and you begin to vent. You leave the conversation angry and feeling down about your own relationship when in reality there is nothing wrong with it.

Now that we have red flags covered, let's move onto the green flags. These are the characteristics you see in people whom you definitely want in your life. The people who possess these infectious characteristics generally have a particular type of demeanour. You will feel a positive vibe from them the moment you meet them. Naturally, this often brings out the best in you, drawing out your own good qualities.

A characteristic green flag could be self-assurance. Surrounding yourself with someone who is self-assured will lead you to become more confident and positive in your own thoughts and ideas, just as they are. Being around a person such as this will lead you to question why you are not like this person; it will start a process within your mind of seeking out the similarities and differences between you and that person, which will drive you to become more like them.

It is important not to be a copycat of someone else but rather to recognise characteristics you do not yet have that will help you on your journey. Life is too short to waste your valuable time with the wrong people. This can be a significant contributor to why many find themselves going off course and the more successful you become, the more selective you have to be and the closer your circle will become.

The hardest thing you'll have to do is letting go of, or at least reducing your time spent with, people who have this negative impact on you. It doesn't mean they are bad people; it's just that they are not on the same journey as you. Sometimes you have to love people from a distance. I am not saying you should cut off your family members and all your friends, but at some point you may need to be mindful of how many hours you are spending with a certain person. Reanalyse the amount of time you spend with the negative 'red flag' people in your life, as they will not push you on your way to reaching your goals.

Ask yourself these questions: 'How often have I spent time with people that I know (and knew at the time) aren't good for me?

Did I only spend time with them because I didn't want to hurt their feelings? Have I ever been in a situation where I have made plans with someone but didn't really want to go, without knowing the real reason why, and therefore made an excuse and put it off?' The answer to this final question may be very clear. It may be your intuition telling you that this person is not good for you and that they are not helping you on your way to achieving your goal(s) in life.

Be a giver (to a certain extent)

It is good to be a giver. It is good to be generous. However, a giver who gives too much can be left with empty pockets.

Let's say that your friend needs your help. He is demotivated, lacks ambition, is feeling down and seems to be spiralling into a black hole. You, being you, want to help as much as you can. You give him advice on the best books to read to boost his mood, along with advice on audio books, speakers, and YouTube clips to watch and listen to. You give him advice on how to better his life in his job and his relationship, and he goes away seeming motivated and inspired. A week later you check in on him and he is back to square one; he feels the same way he felt before he spoke to you initially and has followed none of your advice. Therefore, you, again being you, give him further advice. And the pattern repeats, again and again. But what happens in the end?

You have given him every bit of advice you can think of. And instead of walking away as the positive, motivated individual you are, you feel drained and negative as if you have let him down. You feel guilt when in reality this person has not followed one piece of advice you have given them. RED FLAG. This is not the sort of person who should regularly have access to you. They may be your friend, and you may want to help them as much as you can, but they will drain the positivity out of you.

Think of it like this. You have a circle. It is filled with positivity. When you work on your own projects you take positivity from the circle and inject it into the work you are doing. You reap the rewards, whether it be money or gratitude, and positivity is put back into the circle.

However, whilst helping your friend, you are taking this positivity from your circle and pushing it into him. He is then doing nothing with it, which means there is no positivity to put back into your circle. Your circle becomes smaller and more deflated and, in the end, there is no positivity left for you.

Remember this: you are not responsible for other people's happiness; you are only responsible for your own.

Exercise: Red and Green Flags

This exercise may seem a bit cruel, but there is a reason behind it. Take the five people whom you spend the most time with. Analyse their red flag characteristics and their green flag characteristics. Is it skewed on one side for any of these people? Those who are skewed mostly to the green flag side are those with whom you should be spending most of your time. These are the driven people who will help push you towards your goals.

This is – and I'm not going to lie to you – going to be a horrible process. Analysing your best friends can be heart-breaking if you realise that in reality they are not the best people to associate with. And this is why I must stress again: I AM NOT ASKING YOU TO CUT OFF YOUR FRIENDS COMPLETELY. I'm just asking you to reanalyse the amount of time you spend with people based on the extent to which they will help you to achieve your goals.

Examples:

Red Flags: cynical, lazy, unambitious, uninspired, dishonest, selfish, closed-minded, unreliable, ignorant, immoral, jealous, pessimistic, etc.

Green Flags: ambitious, inspired, honest, giving, open-minded, reliable, moral, optimistic, empowering, committed, self-aware, courageous.

Below is a worksheet that can be printed five times to complete this exercise (if you wish to do it on paper), or it can be completed in your own personal journal.

Person _____

Red Flags: Green Flags:

_____   _____

_____   _____

_____   _____

_____   _____

_____   _____

_____   _____

_____   _____

_____   _____

_____   _____

_____   _____

_____   _____

_____   _____

_____   _____

_____   _____

_____   _____

_____   _____

_____   _____

_____   _____

Accountability

One thing that goes hand in hand with keeping the right company is your level of accountability. If you are around people that are serious about setting and achieving goals, then they will be likely to check in with you on how your goals are progressing.

Being held accountable is an extremely positive thing when you are around the right people. If you do not do something that you said you would, you are not only letting yourself down, you are also letting someone else down.

A powerful action you can take is to get yourself an accountability partner or group. Finding an accountability partner will likely be easier and will assist in keeping you, and them, on track. Find someone that is likeminded and will pull you up when you're not doing what you said you would.

There should be a mutual respect and trust between you both and, once you find that partner, it becomes incredibly exciting to know that, not only are you holding yourself accountable, someone that has your best interests at heart is also doing so.

You can arrange a weekly, biweekly or even monthly check in with each other where you share what goals you are working on, your reflections over the last month and the progress you have made since your last call.

Don't worry if you do not find an accountability partner straight away. You should be motivated enough by your goals to be accountable to yourself.

If you want to go far in life then you set goals, but if you want to go further then you add accountability.

'Beware of the company you keep. See that you associate with the right type of people.'

—Dada Vaswani

12

What Is In It for You and Why?

I n this section it is important to clearly identify what is in it for you and why. When you know your 'why' – when you know deep down the reason for the goal – you will push through the hurdles and the roadblocks without them having a significant impact on your motivation.

The main benefit I have found from this process is that it gives me clarity as to why I am trying to reach this goal, and this gives me the extra momentum I need to get there. Just wanting something isn't a good enough reason to try to obtain it; whereas a completely clear and specific reason in your mind will enable you to overcome most obstacles on your path. Sometimes you may even find that the goal isn't as important to you as you first thought, which saves you wasting a lot of time chasing a goal that in fact you do not really want.

Exercise: 10 reasons why

I use this exercise myself to help me differentiate between goals I really want to achieve and fabricated goals I only think I want to meet.

Write out ten reasons why you want to achieve this goal, and ten things that are 'in it for you' when you get there. The first few will be easy, but as you go along, you might find that you have to spend longer than you expected on completing this task.

Why do I want to achieve this goal?

1. _____

_____

2. _____

_____

3. _____

_____

4. _____

_____

5. _____

_____

6. _____

_____

7. _____

_____

8. _____

_____

9. _____

_____

10. _____

_____

What is in it for me?

1. _____

_____

2. _____

_____

3. _____

_____

4. _____

_____

5. _____

_____

6. _____

_____

7. _____

_____

8. _____

_____

9. _____

_____

10. _____

_____

Do you want a Lamborghini? If you were presented with £300,000 today, would you go to the dealer right away or would you stop and think 'what do I actually want?' The majority of people want to show everyone what their goals are to impress people they don't like. Not every person wants a supercar or a Rolex or a penthouse in central London.

Others have goals such as being free of the "nine to five", having more time to spend with their children, more time to play golf with friends, or just wanting to build businesses. Your values are perfect for you and there is really no need to set goals to impress others. The most refreshing thing you can feel is to filter out the goals that are truly important to you. You'll feel a sense of clarity and have extra motivation to succeed.

Example: Shaun used to find it difficult to achieve his goals. He felt the goals he was focusing on were to impress others, which left him lacking the necessary motivation to push himself towards them. After becoming frustrated that he was not getting to where he needed, there came a moment of enlightenment. He sat down in a quiet place and started to think and have honest conversations with himself. He came to a realisation that he was doing it for the wrong reasons.

Initially, he thought what he wanted was to own a sports car, specifically an Audi R8. But when he sat down and really thought about it, he realised this was not aligned with his core values: it was a goal he had imposed upon himself as a result of feeling he needed to impress others. He came to the realisation that what he was more interested in was reinvesting the capital he had already earned into further building his business, and that he would prefer to spend any remaining cash on living a healthy and active lifestyle. He was much more able to answer the questions 'why do I want to achieve this goal' and 'what's in it for me' when he could identify specific goals that meant more to him.

I cannot stress highly enough how much you need to have clarity with your 'whys'. They need to be at the forefront of your mind.

Your 'whys' need to be bigger than the hurdles you may face, otherwise you will not overcome them. If you have ever felt like this, frustrated in the past with your goals, and may have even felt stuck as to why you're not pushing through, most of the time it's because you haven't considered why you truly want to achieve the goal.

'When you have clarity of intention,
the universe conspires with you
to make it happen.'

—Fabienne Fredrickson

13

What Are You Prepared to Give Up?

I dentifying what you are prepared to give up is key within the goal-setting and goal-achieving process. This is where many people fall down, as they are unprepared to sacrifice in order to achieve the goal they have set.

If you are saving for the deposit of your first home, or any other goal, it is likely you will have to sacrifice holidays, going out with your friends, cinema trips, eating out with your partner, new clothes and any other luxury expenditure on yourself. For some, this sacrifice of enjoyment and treating oneself is too much, which is why they do not achieve their goal of owning their own home, or why it takes them far longer to raise the capital for the deposit than they initially planned.

It's not just about sacrificing money and spending money; it's also about time. There are only twenty four hours in the day, seven days in the week, and fifty-two weeks in the year. You will need to be prepared to reduce the amount of time you spend doing other things in order to achieve your goals.

Example: Shaun works full-time. He works a nine to five job, five days a week, and it takes him approximately an hour to travel to work and home so he is out of the house for 10 hours of the day. He then sleeps for seven hours a night. That is already 17 hours of the day and 99 hours of a 168-hour week gone. Shaun likes to go to the gym, so he spends one and a half hours five times a week exercising. There are now only 61 and a half hours of the week remaining. He spends two hours each day showering and preparing his food and eating. Now there are 47 and a half hours left. He spends six hours at a social event with his friends, seven hours (approx. one hour a day) on social media, 14 hours (approx. two hours a day) watching TV with his partner, five hours on an evening out with his partner for dinner and to the cinema, six hours on a Saturday and Sunday spending time with his family, going for lunch with his partner, going to the beach/shopping/etc, and finally 3.5 hours a week practising his guitar. This is all his time used up.

	M	T	W	T	F	S	S	Total
Work	8	8	8	8	8			40
Travel	2	2	2	2	2			10
Sleep	7	7	7	7	7	7	7	49
Gym	1.5	1.5	1.5	1.5			1.5	7.5
Survival	2	2	2	2	2	2	2	14
Social event						6		6
Social media	1	1	1	1		1	2	7
TV	2	2	2	2		2	4	14
Out with girlfriend					5			5
Family Time/Shopping						6	6	12
Practicing Guitar	0.5	0.5	0.5	0.5			1.5	2.5
Total	24	24	24	24	24	24	24	168

Shaun wants to set up a side business in order to raise capital to buy himself and his partner their first home. He has recognised that he needs to be more efficient with his time as he will need to dedicate time to setting up and growing his business. He has consciously made the decision to:

- reduce his TV time by the equivalent of one hour per day,
- reduce the time he spends on social media weekly to just two hours on the weekend,
- sacrifice social events with his friends three times a month, now only going to one event every four weeks.
- only go out with his partner for dinners and to the cinema every other week. Instead, they will spend three hours getting a takeaway and watching a film.
- dedicate two hours every Saturday and Sunday in the morning to working on his business, as four hours on each of the two days is still quite a lot of time in which to go and see his family and go out with his partner for the afternoon.

On the weeks he is not out with his partner or his friends, he has freed up:

TV time -   7 hours
Social media -   5 hours
Social event -   6 hours
Weekend -   4 hours
Night in -   2 hours
Total -   24 hours

	M	T	W	T	F	S	S	Total
Work	8	8	8	8	8			40
Travel	2	2	2	2	2			10
Sleep	7	7	7	7	7	7	7	49
Gym	1.5	1.5	1.5	1.5		1.5		7.5
Survival	2	2	2	2	2	2	2	14
Social event								0
Social media						1	1	2
TV	1	1	1	1		1	2	7
Takeaway & Film					3			3
Family Time/Shopping						4	4	8
Practicing Guitar	0.5	0.5	0.5	0.5			1.5	2.5
Work on Business	**2**	**2**	**2**	**2**	**2**	**7.5**	**6.5**	**24**
Total	24	24	24	24	24	24	24	168

He has now freed up the equivalent of one day per week in which he can focus on his side business.

On the weeks he is out with his partner, but with his friends, he has freed up:

TV time-   7 hours
Social media -   5 hours
Social event -   6 hours
Weekend -   4 hours
Total -   22 hours

	M	T	W	T	F	S	S	Total
Work	8	8	8	8	8			40
Travel	2	2	2	2	2			10
Sleep	7	7	7	7	7	7	7	49
Gym	1.5	1.5	1.5	1.5		1.5		7.5
Survival	2	2	2	2	2	2	2	14
Social event								0
Social media						1	1	2
TV	1	1	1	1		1	2	7
Out with Girlfriend					5			5
Family Time/Shopping						4	4	8
Practicing Guitar	0.5	0.5	0.5	0.5			1.5	2.5
Work on Business	2	2	2	2	0	7.5	6.5	22
Total	24	24	24	24	24	24	24	168

On the weeks he is not out with his partner, but out with his friends, he has freed up:

TV time -   7 hours
Social media -   5 hours
Weekend -   4 hours
Night in -   2 hours
Total -   18 hours

	M	T	W	T	F	S	S	Total
Work	8	8	8	8	8			40
Travel	2	2	2	2	2			10
Sleep	7	7	7	7	7	7	7	49
Gym	1.5	1.5	1.5	1.5			1.5	7.5
Survival	2	2	2	2	2	2	2	14
Social event						6		0
Social media						1	1	2
TV	1	1	1	1		1	2	7
Takeaway & Film					3			3
Family Time/Shopping						4	4	8
Practicing Guitar	0.5	0.5	0.5	0.5			1.5	2.5
Work on Business	**2**	**2**	**2**	**2**	**2**	**3**	**5**	**18**
Total	24	24	24	24	24	24	24	168

On the weeks he is out with his partner and out with his friends, he has freed up:

TV time -	7 hours
Social media -	5 hours
Weekend -	4 hours
Total -	16 hours

	M	T	W	T	F	S	S	Total
Work	8	8	8	8	8			40
Travel	2	2	2	2	2			10
Sleep	7	7	7	7	7	7	7	49
Gym	1.5	1.5	1.5	1.5			1.5	7.5
Survival	2	2	2	2	2	2	2	14
Social event						6		0
Social media						1	1	2
TV	1	1	1	1		1	2	7
Out with Girlfriend					5			3
Family Time/Shopping						4	4	8
Practicing Guitar	0.5	0.5	0.5	0.5			1.5	2.5
Work on Business	**2**	**2**	**2**	**2**	**0**	**3**	**5**	**16**
Total	24	24	24	24	24	24	24	168

Even in his worst-case scenario week, where he is spending eleven hours out with his friends and his partner, he is still able to free up sixteen hours to work on his business.

It's highly likely that one of the main reasons you're not achieving your goals is the excuses you're telling yourself. Have you ever said to yourself 'oh, I just don't have the time'? Well, the example above shows that most of you WILL have the time. Efficiently managing your time can free up more spare time than you think; it's just a matter of making the sacrifices required in order to do so.

Exercise: Cutting your time

Below is an exercise that divides life into its main sections. Fill in how much time you spend per week on each activity and you'll soon see how much free time you really have.

How I spend my time now (fill in blanks with other time-consuming activities):

	M	T	W	T	F	S	S	Total
Work								
Travel								
Sleeping								
Food/Food Prep								
Showering/Dressing								
Out (Friends)								
Out (Partner)								
Family Time								
TV								
Housework								

How I want to/will now spend my time (fill in blanks with other time-consuming activities):

	M	T	W	T	F	S	S	Total
Work								
Travel								
Sleeping								
Food/Food Prep								
Showering/Dressing								
Out (Friends)								
Out (Partner)								
Family Time								
TV								
Housework								

I understand that sacrifice is hard, but if you are not willing to cut back on the non-essentials then it's going to make achieving your goals more difficult, particularly if they are time-consuming.

Sacrifice is absolutely necessary to get where you want to be in life. Whether that be financially, physically, spiritually or any other way, sacrifice is key. Any role model you have ever looked up to will have had to sacrifice time, pleasure and numerous other things at some point or many points in their life to get where they are. If you want to follow in their footsteps and achieve success in all areas of your life, then you need something that is going to give you your edge.

Many people overcomplicate this; however, the simple practical step above will help you to see what you really spend your time on. Many of you will be surprised at how much time you spend doing nothing. You may even be struggling to fill in the full twenty-four hours of the day as you're sometimes unaware of how you are really spending your time.

Imagine if you could give yourself a day – a full day a week – as Shaun did to work towards your goal. Picture how quickly it would become a reality. A whole twenty-four hours a week, for fifty-two weeks of the year, is a massive 1,248 hours a year to work towards your goal. Now tell me you 'don't have the time'. Ask yourself 'how many goals are achievable within those hours?'

Offset your time

One good way to save time would be to multitask. If you don't want to give up either going to the gym or reading/listening to books, a good idea would be to combine them. Whilst in the gym, whether you are doing weights or on the treadmill, it would be time-efficient to listen to your audio book at the same time. (This would also work for housework.) Do you drive or use public transport to get to work? Would it be more time-efficient for you to get the train so you can reply to emails during the time in which you would usually be driving? The key point here is that offsetting your time can make your day much more productive.

'If you don't sacrifice for what you want,
what you want will be the sacrifice.'

—Unknown

14

Affirmations

Affirmations boost your vibrational frequency and have the ability to rewire your brain. This is a small yet effective step in the process of setting and achieving your goals. In the earlier section on psychology, you saw what affirmations are and how the vocabulary used can be very influential on the effectiveness of this process. However, when setting goals, it is extremely important to ensure your stated affirmations link closely to your goals. Although affirmations such as 'I attract an abundance of health, wealth and happiness' can be highly effective in general life, if you have the specific goal of achieving 10% body fat, it is only loosely linked to the subject.

If you really want to be in the state of flow, then it is ideal to include affirmations in your daily routine. The average human has 60-70 thousand thoughts every day. 90% of those thoughts will be exactly the same the next day. Science shows us that there is a very high chance we will consistently have the same thoughts about ourselves tomorrow as we did today, unless we change the words we say today which in turn will change how we think tomorrow.

So whether you believe in affirmations or not, you are either affirming good things to yourself or bad things to yourself. Being aware of your thoughts is one of the most effective ways of training yourself to produce positive outcomes.

> *"Watch your thoughts, they become your words.*
> *Watch your words, they become your actions.*
> *Watch your actions, they become your habits. Watch*
> *your habits, they become your character. Watch*
> *your character, for it becomes your destiny."*
>
> *– Lao Tzu*

Studies have shown that if you say something out loud it is 10 times more powerful than your thoughts. In addition to this, negativity is 4 to 7 times more powerful than positivity.

Think about that.

If you say a negative comment out loud you increase its probability of happening by 40 to 70 times more than if you hadn't said anything at all.

This is the hidden power of words and thoughts that most people don't even realise. And, by understanding their power, positive and negative, it's too much of a risk not to be aware of the words you speak every day. If you truly want to change your life, then it starts with changing your words.

Your life is manifesting exactly how you are describing it.

Example: Shaun is very fitness-orientated. He has the goal of achieving 10% body fat and then maintaining a lean and toned physique. The most effective way to affirm this would be to write it down in this manner:

I am 10% body fat on or before 1 December 2021.
I am 10% body fat on or before 1 December 2021.

I am 10% body fat on or before 1 December 2021.
I am 10% body fat on or before 1 December 2021.
I am 10% body fat on or before 1 December 2021.
I am 10% body fat on or before 1 December 2021.
I am 10% body fat on or before 1 December 2021.
I am 10% body fat on or before 1 December 2021.
I am 10% body fat on or before 1 December 2021.
I am 10% body fat on or before 1 December 2021.

I do 30 minutes of cardio training every day.
I do 30 minutes of cardio training every day.
I do 30 minutes of cardio training every day.
I do 30 minutes of cardio training every day.
I do 30 minutes of cardio training every day.
I do 30 minutes of cardio training every day.
I do 30 minutes of cardio training every day.
I do 30 minutes of cardio training every day.
I do 30 minutes of cardio training every day.
I do 30 minutes of cardio training every day.

I am strong, lean, toned and feel in great shape.
I am strong, lean, toned and feel in great shape.
I am strong, lean, toned and feel in great shape.
I am strong, lean, toned and feel in great shape.
I am strong, lean, toned and feel in great shape.
I am strong, lean, toned and feel in great shape.
I am strong, lean, toned and feel in great shape.
I am strong, lean, toned and feel in great shape.
I am strong, lean, toned and feel in great shape.
I am strong, lean, toned and feel in great shape.

As already mentioned in the psychology section, writing out the affirmations ten times solidifies them in your mind, focusing you further on your goal and giving you a higher likelihood of staying on track and therefore achieving your goals. This step comes at the very end of the fully written-out goal. After all of the previous eight steps have been completed fully, this is an added bonus to ensure you're moving in the right direction and doing everything within your power to achieve your goal.

You don't need to use the affirmations I've provided; you can make up your own but you need to ensure they are positively written in the way explained in the psychology section of this book.

Tip: It is important to be visually connected to the words you are saying. If your affirmation is "I am a confident public speaker" it is important to visualise yourself standing on a stage, speaking publicly and confidently., as you say these words to yourself.

Seven-Day Affirmation Challenge

This is a really easy way to get you going, especially if you've never done affirmations before, and it's a fast way to create a habit. Commit yourself to writing down a minimum of five affirmations, five times, every single day. This will soon become a part of your routine and you'll quickly begin to see a difference in how you think and feel.

Exercise: Take one of your goals and think of two specific and relevant affirmations that apply. Write them out in the correct format and language, keeping them positive and in the present.

Goal:

_____

_____

Affirmation 1:

1._____

_____

2._____

_____

3._____

_____

4._____

_____

5._____

_____

6._____

_____

7._____

_____

8._____

_____

9._____

_____

10._____

_____

Affirmation 2:

1._____

_____

2._____

_____

3._____

_____

4._____

_____

5._____

_____

6._____

_____

7._____

_____

8._____

_____

9._____

_____

10._____

_____

'Affirmation without discipline is the beginning of delusion.'

—Jim Rohn

15

Visualisation

Visualisation is the process of engaging your senses in order to make the goal feel closer and more real. I like to think of it as a type of meditation, where you are focusing your mind completely on your goal and visualising that the goal has already been achieved. It is an essential way to get in touch with your goal on a more intimate level. I have personally used visualisation whilst setting the goal of writing this book. I imagined and pictured this book before I began writing it, and today here you are reading it.

Visualisation can be used to programme your mind and body into achieving positive results. It has been said that visualisation and the mind hold an important role in the creation of experiences, and therefore the positive experiences created through visualisation can be the driving force to achieving your goals.

It is a form of rehearsal of your goal, mentally imagining the goal multiple times and rehearsing the feeling in your mind. Certain studies, such as Emotional Memory Management: Positive Control Over Your Memory by Joseph M. Carver, Ph.D., have shown that the brain doesn't know the difference between imagining something and actually doing it. In his work, Carver found that basketball players who practised shots for one month improved their skill by 24%, while those who only mentally imagined practising their shots improved by 23% and those who did nothing did not improve.

Think of this in relation to your goals, and your future. If you are actively visualising your future and how you want it to be, you brain won't distinguish between you imagining it and it actually having happened. And so you your subconscious will begin to steer you in the direction of that future.

Now imagine your goal. Whether it is to be able to make twenty basketball shots in a row, have 10% body fat, own a Ferrari, or be a great businessperson, really imagine it. Picture it in your mind and your body will instinctively begin to work towards this target without your conscious control. You'll find yourself working harder in the gym or feeling more motivated to finish business plans and set up meetings with potential investors, because your body and mind will already know what it feels like to be in that shape or to be that successful.

The five-minute rule

The most basic method of visualisation would be through five minutes of meditation. For five minutes every evening before you go to bed, ensure that you have some time to yourself. Begin to visualise yourself as the person who has already achieved that goal. Imagine looking at yourself in the mirror as an athletic individual, or picture looking down at yourself in a sharp suit on the way to your international business meeting. Whatever your goal is, visualise it.

Then again, for the first five minutes after you wake, repeat this process. Visualise exactly how your life will be when you have achieved this goal and visualise the happiness you will feel when you get there. This will be the strongest push you need towards your goals.

Get your senses involved

Visualising can sometimes be difficult if you have not experienced the particular sensation before. The best thing to do to overcome this difficulty is to get your senses involved.

Example: Shaun has always dreamed of owning a Porsche GT3. As he has never sat in or driven one he is finding it difficult to visualise what it would be like to own one.

Therefore, he first uses YouTube to listen to the sound a Porsche GT3 makes, then closes his eyes whilst sitting in his own car and listens to the sound of the rev of the engine, imagining that he is sitting in a Porsche GT3.

He then imagines the smell of the Porsche GT3. Does it have a new car smell? Does it smell like a particular air freshener? He goes out to buy that air freshener and puts it in his own car.

Next, he visits the Porsche garage to sit in and see and feel the car for himself.

With all this newfound knowledge of the car, it is easier for Shaun to use his five minutes and accurately visualise owning the car for himself.

With the information from the 'Detail is Key' chapter, visualisation can be a simple but effective technique in bringing your goal closer to you. You have already stated specifically what your goal is and described every aspect in great detail; now use this information to picture it in your mind.

While you are reading this, take part in a small task for me.

Raise your hand.
Now raise it higher.
And now higher again.
And now even higher.

Why did you not raise it that high in the first place? When I first asked you to raise your hand, why did you not raise it as high as possible?

It's almost as if your initial thought as to where you believe yourself to be is lower. Why did you not feel comfortable enough the first time to raise your hand as high as you could? Visualisation helps to continually push through the barriers of your belief system, helping you to imagine life in a greater way than you could before, breaking through that self-imposed threshold.

Exercise: Meditation and visualisation

Although five minutes of meditation can be somewhat effective in enabling you to achieve your goals, the more you are able to visualise the better.

Take your five senses: sight, touch, taste, sound and smell. Pick four of them (I understand that taste can be difficult to apply to many goals) and choose four ways in which you can engage your senses to better visualise your goal.

Example for Shaun and his car:

- Sight - go to a showroom and see the car. Look through the catalogues and select colours, specific features and add-ons that I would want on my car.
- Touch - sit in the car in the showroom and feel the steering wheel, gearstick, hand brake; press the pedals and be as hands-on as possible whilst sitting in the car.
- Sound - listen to the sound on YouTube or take the car for a test drive or be driven around by the dealer.
- Smell - smell the new car smell or the smell of the air freshener; then go out and buy the air freshener and put it in the car.

After you have completed these four steps you will be able to involve the majority of your senses whilst you are visualising. I would recommend visualisation for fifteen minutes per day and also that you go through each sense separately, picturing the sensations felt for each one.

Goal:

_____

_____

Sense 1: _____

_____

_____

_____

Sense 2: _____

_____

_____

_____

Sense 3: _____

_____

_____

_____

Sense 4: _____

_____

_____

_____

Exercise: the Cinema Technique

Close your eyes and imagine you are on your own in the cinema. Step out of your body, float up and look down on yourself from a bird's-eye view now watching the film. Onscreen is a black and white film about your ideal life. Now imagine what your ideal life is like or how you want it to be. Who is in this life? Do you have a husband/wife? Do you have children? What do you look like? What do they look like?

Then look more deeply into your own character. How do you stand/talk/walk? How are you dressed? How do your husband/wife and children behave? What are they like? What type of car do you drive and what type of house do you live in? What job are you in, or are you self-employed or a business owner?

Now turn your black and white picture into colour. What colour is your car? What colour is your house? How do others perceive you? Do you have lots of friends? Go further into the details of your life and be extremely specific.

Now imagine you come back down into your body, feeling present and centred.

This could take you five to ten minutes and I would encourage you to do it once a week, or even once a day, depending on how in touch with your goal you want to be.

By performing this exercise, you have done something extremely powerful. You're bringing your goal into the forefront of your mind whilst anchoring it in your subconscious.

Through this technique of visualisation, you will be able to incorporate this ideal version of your life into your own. You will begin to walk, talk and act like the man/woman in your film. You will be motivated to be, and will slowly become, the person from your ideal life.

A day in the life

If you could live your life as if you had already achieved your goal, what would it be like? A potential exercise you can do is to take one random day off work and spend it the way you would if your life existed as you had visualised. This is a deeper way to visualise the achievement of your goal, as you are behaving and feeling exactly what it would be like.

This was a particular exercise I found very useful whilst employed. I would take a day off midweek and spend it in the way I envisioned my life would be. I would get up in the morning, hit the gym, trade whilst in a coffee shop and work on my businesses, which at that point were just at the idea stage. I found this an extremely helpful exercise as it confirmed to me that this was really what I wanted to do with my life and solidified my goal. I remember thinking to myself 'if I had this much time free every day, imagine what I could achieve in one week, let alone one year'.

Rather than fantasise over a goal that you would like to happen, do something out of the ordinary that 99% of people just won't do. The more you perform the day in the life exercise, the more you will increase the connection towards believing in yourself. No longer will they be 'nice to have' goals, you'll actually solidify the inner belief that they will be a reality.

'If you can see it in your mind,
you can hold it in your hand.'

—Bob Proctor

16

Reflection

Although not an actual step in the goal setting process, reflection is key when tracking how far you have come in relation to achieving your goals. This is something I have been doing for years and I have found it exceptionally helpful in keeping me focused and on track with my goals. I've personally found that reflections have been very useful when looking back on the goals I have set.

What is self-reflection?

Self-reflection is like looking into a mirror and describing what you see. It is a way of assessing yourself, your ways of working, your ways of progression, and helps you identify what you could improve on in the future.

Why is self-reflection key?

Reflecting helps you to review the development of your skills. It helps you figure out if you have stuck to your original plan and how you can make sure you continue to do so for the coming months or begin to do so if you haven't already. In any role, whether at home or at work, reflection is an important part of learning. You wouldn't use a recipe a second time around if the dish didn't work the first time, you would either scrap it or you would alter the recipe until you have the right ingredients to create something special.

Reflective questions you can ask yourself:

- Strengths – What are my strengths? For example, am I good at leading? Am I punctual?
- Weaknesses – What are my weaknesses? For example, do I lack focus? Am I always late for appointments?
- Skills – What skills do I have and what am I good at? Am I good at organisation?
- Problems – What problems are there in my life, whether home- or work-related, that I can work on right now?
- Achievements – What have I achieved in the last month? Have I created two sources of income? Have I graduated from university?
- Happiness – Are there things that I am unhappy with or disappointed about? Are there things that have made me really happy? For example: weight, freedom, creating business.
- Solutions – How can I improve these areas of my life and what can I do now to work towards this?

Self-reflection can be difficult because it requires you being honest with yourself, which a lot of people don't like to do. But the more you do it, the easier it will be to get honest with yourself. This is self-awareness and it can be the fastest way to admit to yourself what you need to do or how to change in order to get closer to your goals.

Reflection isn't just about looking back – it's also there to show you how to look forward, with an end result of giving you more clarity in your life and feeling happier overall.

Exercise: Goal-specific reflective questions

When reflecting on the goals I have set, I find that asking myself the following questions helps keep me on track. Go back and pick each goal you have set in turn, and use these questions weekly/monthly/quarterly, or however frequently you wish, to see if you have kept yourself on track.

Goal: _____

_____

Question: What have I done since my last reflection that has pushed me closer to achieving my goal?

1._____

_____

2._____

_____

3._____

_____

4._____

_____

5._____

_____

Question: Have I encountered any hurdles since my last reflection? If so, what were they?

1._____

_____

2._____

_____

3._____

_____

4._____

_____

5._____

_____

Question: How did I overcome this hurdle?

1._____

_____

2._____

_____

3._____

_____

4._____

_____

5._____

_____

Question: How much closer am I to my goal?

_____

_____

_____

_____

Question: What can I do this month that will push me further in the right direction?

1._____

_____

2._____

_____

3._____

_____

4._____

_____

5._____

_____

Example: Shaun loves business and fitness, and his goal is to own and run his own gym. He set his goal a month ago and wants to look back on what he has done over the past month to project himself towards his goal. He has already written out his goal in detail and has read it over again before completing this task. It's now time to check in with himself to see how far he has come.

Goal: I own and run my own gym on or before 31 December 2021

Question: What have I done since my last reflection that has pushed me closer to achieving my goal?

1. I have enrolled on a personal training course to increase my knowledge about fitness and learn the techniques required to train others.
2. I have written up a full business plan with budgets and savings targets for the next twelve months to ensure I have the capital to lease the building; this includes an average of all monthly outgoings, including lease of machines.

Question: Have I encountered any hurdles since my last reflection?

If so, what were they?

1. The property that I was initially hoping would be available will not be out of lease until March 2023.
2. One of the investors has pulled out for personal reasons and I now need to raise more funds.

Question: How did I overcome this hurdle?

1. I have researched other buildings in the same area to find other potential venues.
2. I have attended an event where the main goal was to bring start-ups and potential investors together.

Question: How much closer am I to my goal?

So far I have ticked off fifteen out of a hundred of the manageable steps on my way to achieving my goal. Therefore, I am 15% of the way through and I am seriously motivated to continue to tick off more. My target is to achieve this goal within the next 12 months and if I continue to tick off fifteen tasks per month it will take me 6.7 months to achieve my goal. Therefore, I am on track.

Question: What can I do this month that will push me further in the right direction?

1. I will structure my day more effectively so that I am more efficient with my time and can complete more tasks within the next month.
2. I will work on more effective ways to market the gym to reach a wider audience, such as emailing those who may be interested in joining on launch.

I have provided two examples for each of the goal-specific reflection questions but would recommend more. You can see from this example how ticking off the small manageable steps can help to motivate and drive you on your way to reaching your goal. Most people don't realise this and are surprised by how much further on they are when they simply reflect on the past weeks and months. Ticking off your manageable steps day-by-day and week-by-week and reviewing them regularly ensures you remain on track. By checking in with yourself monthly and seeing how far you have already come, it can make the initial goal seem less daunting.

I personally reflect at the end of each month as I feel this gives me a substantial amount of time in which to fully complete a number of those manageable steps and I can see a greater progression in the number of steps that have been ticked off. This leads to twelve reflections that I can review fully at the end of the year to see how far I have come over the year as a whole. It is a great personal achievement to be able to see all the things you have ticked off each month. Think what it will be like five years down the line when you have sixty reflections you can look at to see how much you have grown.

The Twelve Reflections

Imagine having twelve reflections for the whole year to look back on and reading how you felt in those moments. Some of the moments may be certain months in which you had a breakthrough or achieved one of your major goals. The important thing here is looking back and reading your reflections from January to December. This holds more of a sentimental value but is also still a very important part of your journey and is why I encourage you to do at least twelve reflections a year, one at the end of every month, to see how far you have come.

'Without deep reflection, one knows from daily life that one exists for other people.'

—Albert Einstein

17

The Side Effect

At this point you should be clear about which goals you want to achieve and have set them accordingly. If you are still going through a draft and don't feel like you are 100% set on your goals, that is fine. It will become clearer the more you go back over the process.

In life, it is normal to want to keep striving to achieve more goals. There will come a point in time where you may lose a connection to your goals. After all, the process of who we become can be more important than the goal itself.

One of the biggest shifts in mindset that has enabled me to take my achievements to a new level is something I call 'The Side Effect'.

The Side Effect is more commonly used with materialistic/have goals. It is the process of rewarding yourself with a materialistic goal you aim to achieve after you have achieved a 'be' or 'do' goal.

The novelty can wear off when achieving more materialistic, tangible goals. All of the excitement you have built up for the goal may result in an anti-climax when the goal is finally achieved. I found this happening myself, that the goals started to lose meaning and it became more about the chase for the goal itself rather than the end result.

This is where the side effect comes in. I began linking my goals together, so that each set or group of goals had a more personal and emotional attachment. This actually gave me an even deeper drive and passion to want to achieve a new goal that I set.

I had a dream, like many of you may do, to build my parents a house within my own property boundary and take care of them financially. When I first set the goal to provide my parents a house, many years ago, I told myself that in order for me to achieve this, it's going to take a big push for me to be in a position to do so. In the midst of all of this I had some other personal goals that I desired. However, in recent times I found myself in a position where I was financially able to tick most of them off, which almost lacked meaning.

Over the last few years, I have realised that thinking about my personal rewards as a 'side effect' of achieving other goals, such as the goal for my parents, gave me a stronger connection to the more materialistic goal and pushed me to a whole new level of motivation.

It was for this reason that I rewarded myself with one of my personal, materialistic goals as a reward for providing my parents with the home I had always dreamed of giving them. This resulted in the 'side effect' having greater meaning for me and removed the anti-climactic feeling when I rewarded myself.

The true benefit of seeing your goals as a side effect is that it involves a total shift in mindset. It is not only liberating but gives you a deeper emotional connection to all of your goals and has the ability to make the goal mean something bigger than the goal itself.

Commit yourself to something
bigger than yourself.

—Jim Rohn

18

Upgrading Your Mindset

Aggressive Patience

We often hear the term "just be patient" which can sometimes be somewhat antagonistic. We have to find the balance between wanting something to happen in an "unrealistic deadline" and having your head in the clouds, saying that you are being patient and hoping for something to happen. This is where aggressive patience will serve you.

Aggressive patience refers to having the ability to be patient with the bigger vision you have set whilst continuing to aggressively and move daily towards your goals while making sure that you are ticking off goals that are congruent with the bigger picture.

Essentially, it involves having the thought process that this bigger vision may take time yet, day by day, you are actively completing the manageable steps to progress towards the end goal.

Becoming the Asset

If your goal is to build long term wealth, or however you have defined your version of success, you should see yourself as becoming the asset. This, again, involves a shift in mindset.

The majority of people will rely their whole life on one source of income and fail to invest their time in learning skills that will provide them with additional expertise in order to generate further wealth.

You 'become the asset' by making yourself valuable in multiple different areas, and if you wish to make that asset more valuable you will need to keep investing your time and energy into developing yourself.

When you have this thought process you will constantly feel empowered. We can spend many years working a job that we do not enjoy just to be let go at the click of a finger.

Not becoming the asset is a far greater risk.

Become an asset or you will become someone else's liability.

The successful warrior is the average man with laserlike focus.

—Bruce Lee

19

Core Values and Daily Goals

On a subconscious level we already have sets of values, whether we are aware of them or not, that we follow in life.

Example: Shaun likes to donate regularly to charity and to help children in need. It is thus likely that one of the values he holds strongly will be giving. This might seem very obvious but sometimes we spend a lifetime trying to work out who we really are when it's actually quite simple.

I have found it helpful to write down every day a list of five values that are most important to me alongside my daily goals. Let me show you.

- Honesty - I am always honest with myself and others and expect the same from my family, social circle and friends.
- Persistent - I persist with the tasks at hand to bring me closer to my goals.
- Passionate - I am passionate about my goals and love what I am working on.

- Caring - I care about my family, friends and myself deeply.
- Laser-focused - I am not just focused but laser-focused, with absolute precision, on my goals.

I write down my values every day as a reminder that they are aligned with my goals. It makes you realise that you are working on the goals that are most important to you.

I spent nearly two years working on goals that I thought were really important to me and I don't regret them for one minute as they have shaped who I am today, and I am truly grateful to be able to understand what I really want out of life.

I want you to make sure that you are being true to yourself, as time is precious and should not be wasted on goals that are unimportant to you. It will not make you happy and will leave you feeling unfulfilled. Identifying your core values is singlehandedly one of the most important things you can do, as it helps shape a more efficient path towards achieving your goals.

If you come to a hurdle and give up on your goal easily, you'll find yourself saying "why can't I follow things through?" or "that goal was just too hard for me and I need to set more REALISTIC targets". This is usually to make yourself feel better and to justify why you haven't achieved the goal, when in fact the reason you haven't succeeded is because the goal was not in alignment with your core values. We all know what realistic thinking will get you… realistic results, and that's not what we want.

You have to dig deep, be honest with yourself and ask the question "if I had no one to impress, or no one to show what I have done, would the goals I am currently working towards really be my goals?"

For example, if your goal was to own a Ferrari, but you lived in the most remote of locations and no one would be around to see it, would you still want the Ferrari? Would you want the Ferrari for yourself, or for the impression it gives others of you? I know this may seem like a strange way to think, but sometimes it is the only way to be honest with yourself. When you figure out what your core values really are and then align them with your goals, you'll find that not only is it more enjoyable but also that hurdles in your way will not faze you, as it will not be a matter of 'if' you achieve your goals but 'when' and any hurdle will just be a minor setback.

List of values to help you pick which are most important to you

Adventure	Affection	Balance
Change	Communication	Community
Culture	Education	Family
Fun	Growth	Happiness
Health	Inspiration	Integrity
Knowledge	Love	Loyalty
Motivation	Patience	Peace
Personal Development	Power	Relationships
Respect	Stability	Success
Travel	Trust	Wealth

From the list I have provided, or from your own values, select the five that most relate to you; the ones that stick out are most likely to be the most important values to you as a person.

Now, with your values in mind, think about what being successful really means to you. Understanding how you define success means you are better able to succeed in turning your dreams into goals and then into reality. Success to you could mean anything from having a happy family, to being financially secure or healthy and fit. Whatever it means, write down those answers in bullet points in your journal.

Exercise 1 – Daily Goals

Write down five goals to achieve every day. These goals needs to be congruent with the bigger vision that you have set for yourself. Start by putting the date at the top followed by your signature, and then your signature again at the bottom right corner of the page.

The reason for this is that when you sign a document, there is a feeling of obligation to fulfil what you have signed. This will have the same effect on you as when you sign your daily goals; you will feel committed.

Five small goals could be as follows.

- go to the gym – push and pull workout
- one hour of reading/audio book
- thirty minutes road running
- one hour writing out goals
- meditate for ten minutes using the Brain.fm app

Tick these goals off as the day goes by and watch the magic happen. When you become accustomed to ticking off these small goals, your mind starts to think 'if I can achieve these, what else can I achieve?"

I like to call this the conditioning process. You are getting your mind ready – essentially building the mental foundations – for achieving bigger goals! Once you get used to achieving the small goals, tackling the bigger goals seems much easier!

Exercise 2 – Daily Values

Write down your daily goals and then list your daily values. Align your values with your goals. This exercise is designed to help you overcome what's holding you back and align you with your goal setting.

Exercise 3 – Affirmations and Signature

After you have listed your goals and values and aligned them with each other, write out affirmations that are going to motivate you to achieve your goals and that are in line with your core values.

Example: Shaun likes to keep fit. Therefore, the following could be an example of his three combined exercises.

Daily Goals:

1. Five-mile run in the morning
2. Spend one hour working on a new blog post
3. Spend one hour writing out my fitness goal in full
4. Go to the gym – push and pull workout
5. Spend one hour reading

Values:

1. Integrity
2. Persistence
3. Passion
4. Health
5. Knowledge

Affirmations:

I persist until I succeed.
I persist until I succeed.
I persist until I succeed.
I persist until I succeed.
I persist until I succeed.
Eating only healthy, nutritious, good food is my lifestyle.
Eating only healthy, nutritious, good food is my lifestyle.
Eating only healthy, nutritious, good food is my lifestyle.
Eating only healthy, nutritious, good food is my lifestyle.
Eating only healthy, nutritious, good food is my lifestyle.
Every goal I strive for I do with passion.
Every goal I strive for I do with passion.

Every goal I strive for I do with passion.
Every goal I strive for I do with passion.
Every goal I strive for I do with passion.
I am 10% body fat with lean muscle on or before 31 Dec 2021.
I am 10% body fat with lean muscle on or before 31 Dec 2021.
I am 10% body fat with lean muscle on or before 31 Dec 2021.
I am 10% body fat with lean muscle on or before 31 Dec 2021.
I am 10% body fat with lean muscle on or before 31 Dec 2021.
I am laser-focused each and every day.
I am laser-focused each and every day.
I am laser-focused each and every day.
I am laser-focused each and every day.
I am laser-focused each and every day.

The 5-5-5 Rule

The above is what I call the 5-5-5 rule. Your mental 5-a-day. Nutrition for the mind.

5 goals.
5 affirmations, each written 5 times.
5 values.

The reason why I focus on the 5-5-5 rule is because of the power of incremental growth. Small daily actions, small growth in each key area of your life, can become so powerful over the longer term because it compounds.

Small daily goals have always been underestimated by the masses. People are often looking for the "secret", the quick fix or the "holy grail" to be able to, almost, cheat the system and achieve their goals without having to truly work for them. But in reality life doesn't work like that. The only thing that we can rely on, that has stood the test of time, is hard work, smart work, and perseverance.

I like to think of goal setting, and goal achieving, like a movie. Has anyone ever told you to "Watch this movie. It's a really slow starter but it gets a lot better"? Think of your goals in the same way. In the beginning it can feel like a slow start – you are ticking off the daily goals, working towards the bigger goals, and it can feel like a very slow process. But it won't be long before you can actively see how far you have come, how much you have progressed towards the bigger vision, and build even more confidence in yourself.

Why?

Sticking to the 5-5-5 rule will keep you focussed, disciplined and intentional in your actions. It is a daily reminder of the manageable steps and a measurement of your commitment towards your goals. It will also serves as a representation of all the hard work you have put into achieving your goals that can be a springboard for future motivation for future goals.

Prioritisation

If you are the sort of person who finds it difficult to get things done in priority order, I highly recommend using colours to direct your eyes towards your most important daily goals.

Put a small circle/box beside each of your goals and fill it with the corresponding colour. Ensure the most important boxes are ticked off first.

Red – high priority, must be done, critical
Orange – moderate priority, needs to be done
Green – low priority, to do but still have time to do it after today

Exercise sheet:

GOALS, VALUES AND AFFIRMATIONS

Date:_____

Daily Goals

1._____

2._____

3._____

4._____

5._____

Daily Values

1._____

2._____

3._____

4._____

5._____

Affirmation 1:

_____

_____

_____

_____

_____

Affirmation 2:

_____

_____

_____

_____

Affirmation 3:

_____

_____

_____

_____

Affirmation 4:

_____

_____

_____

_____

Affirmation 5:

_____

_____

_____

_____

Bonus Exercise:

To ensure that your goals really are aligned with your values, you can use the following sheet.

Daily Goals

1._____

2._____

3._____

4._____

5._____

Daily Values

1._____

2._____

3._____

4._____

5._____

Link – here you should write the reasons why your values and goals are aligned.

Goal _____ links to Value _____ because_____

_____

Goal _____ links to Value _____ because_____

_____

Goal _____ links to Value _____ because_____

_____

Goal _____ links to Value _____ because_____

_____

Goal _____ links to Value _____ because_____

_____

Goal _____ links to Value _____ because_____

_____

Goal _____ links to Value _____ because_____

_____

Goal _____ links to Value _____ because_____

_____

Goal _____ links to Value _____ because_____

_____

Goal _____ links to Value _____ because_____

_____

There could be a particular goal that links to three different values, or one value that links to multiple goals. Fill in as many as possible. This is not an everyday exercise; do it only when you feel you need to confirm to yourself why you are working towards a particular goal.

Example: Shaun

Goal 1 links to Value 4 because to achieve the goal of running every morning, I'll value health.

For this example (Goal 1) Shaun could have chosen persistence, as this value is also aligned with running. This shows that many goals and values will interlink in multiple ways. There will not be just one value that links to a particular goal and vice versa.

'Values are like fingerprints, nobody's are the same, but you leave them all over everything you do.'

—Elvis Presley

20

How to Create the Ultimate Vision Board

M any people underestimate the power of a vision board in achieving their goals. However, having something to physically look at on a daily basis as a reminder of what you are working towards can be a strong motivational force.

Firstly, print off a picture to represent your goal on photographic paper. If your goal is materialistic, then this will be fairly easy, but it may need more thought if it is a 'be' or 'do' goal. The reason for using photographic paper is that standard paper will not make the goal appear as realistic for one particular reason; the former looks like a photo that you yourself could have taken rather than a picture you have printed off yourself. The purpose is to be able to get your mind to believe that you have already achieved the goal before it has happened, so what better way than to have the pictures on your vision board appear to be photos.

This by no means implies that you can simply stick a picture onto a board and it will happen. Of course, you are going to have to work for it and towards it. This process of printing your goal out onto photographic paper needs to be accompanied by some serious action.

Remember: 'A dream with a date becomes a goal'. Having a clearly written out goal, dated, with a vision board can be incredibly powerful to the subconscious mind. The best way to feel the effects and experience it is to do it yourself. Make something to be proud of! Create something that will make you wake up every day and say 'YES! These are my goals and I am doing everything in my power to achieve them.'

Sometimes you just need a boost. It is highly unlikely that a person is positive and feeling the most driven they can be every single day; at the end of the day we are all human. We suffer rejections and setbacks and these can leave us feeling deflated and demotivated – even the most successful people in the world will have a day where they feel 'off'. One issue that has grown significantly over the last 10 years is the use of social media and how it makes people feel inadequate. Social media has been a massive player in the game of trapping people into thinking that the lives of the rich and successful are plain sailing and easy going. They have bad days too – stressful days and bad experiences – but these are the parts you don't see. We are shown only the fancy watches, big houses and sports cars, not the small bite-size chunks people take in order to achieve their goals.

In reality, all goals are just bite-size chunks taken consistently. If you ever feel demotivated or disheartened by the time taken to achieve your goals, then remember: "Water wears the marble."

Step-by-step guide

Here are simple steps to follow to create the ultimate vision board.

STEP 1: Filter and write out your key goals using in your personal journal.

STEP 2: Find/create/buy a vision board. This could be a pin board or white board on which you can stick your pictures as a reminder of what you are aiming to achieve.

STEP 3: Find images that are most applicable to your goal, preferably those that are personal to you. For example, if one of your goals is to own a particular car, rather than just getting an image from the internet head to the dealer and take a picture of yourself in the car you want. Seeing yourself already sitting in the car is far more powerful than seeing a picture of a car you found online.

STEP 4: Print your pictures out on photo paper rather than normal paper.

STEP 5: Sign and date the photograph. This will signal to your brain that you are now obligated to achieve this goal as it will symbolise a contract.

STEP 6: Pin them all onto your vision board to create a collage of all the goals that are most important to you. This will be a constant daily reminder of the hard work you are putting in and of exactly what you are working towards.

STEP 7: Admire daily.

Creating a vision board is actually very simple. Following these steps, you are going to have your own tailored and personal ultimate vision board that is going to drive you towards your goals and remind you daily of what your hard work will result in.

'Create the highest, grandest vision possible for your life because you become what you believe.'

—Oprah Winfrey

21

Summary

Define your vision – Before setting out to achieve any goals, it is important that we first establish a clear vision of what your ideal life would be like. At this stage, it is not about making it 'perfect'. Having a clear vision is what will keep you moving forward over the hurdles you may face. Remember: this is only your first draft.

10 things I want to be, do and have – This process will allow you to filter through the noise of what you 'think' you want and what you 'really' want, leaving you with 30 goals, nine of which ultimately mean the most to you. Remember: not everything you initially write down will be what means the most to you, it may take some time to filter through to what you really want.

Set a date – When setting goals, it is important to have a set date in mind to spur you on, to give you the extra push you need and to keep you on track. Getting closer to your deadline and knowing you've only given yourself an allocated amount of time will keep you focused. Remember: there are no unrealistic goals, only unrealistic deadlines.

Detail is key – Knowing exactly what you want, and writing it out in detail, will be a motivational push for anyone on their way to getting there. There is a big difference between saying 'my goal is to buy a new car' and 'my goal is to own a 2021 Audi R8 that is red with black wheels…' etc. Remember: sign your goals. This will make you feel committed to them, as if you have signed a contract.

Manageable steps – Break down your goal into bite-size chunks. You cannot climb a mountain without taking individual steps. This can help to make your goals feel less daunting. A big goal can feel intimidating at first but breaking it down into manageable pieces can make it seem more attainable. Remember: there needs to be an equilibrium between breaking the steps down too much or too little.

Identify the skills and knowledge required – Could you play in an orchestra without first having learnt to play an instrument? This applies to every goal. There will be set knowledge and skills that are needed to help you on your way to achieving your goal. Once you have identified and begun to work on them, you are one step closer. Remember: a great way to find out the skills and knowledge required is to assess those of your mentors.

Identify your obstacles – Identifying what your potential hurdles are at the beginning can make it easier to overcome them. It will stop you feeling so deflated when you come across one, will keep you on track and will maintain your momentum. Although hurdles can be frustrating, they can be overcome and you can continue on your path to achieving your goal. Remember: in reality, you are your only true obstacle.

People to associate with – You become an accumulation of the five people who occupy most of your time. Look out for the red flags in people who will not further you on your journey to achieving your goals and surround yourself with those who will. 'If you surround yourself with clowns, don't be surprised when your life resembles the circus' (Dr Steve Maraboli). Remember: a giver who gives too much will be left with empty pockets.

What is in it for you and why? – Knowing why you want to achieve your goals gives you more purpose. Your 'why' will be the foundation to continue to push you forward. You also need to work out what's in it for you. Trying to achieve a goal because you want to impress someone else or make them happy will not give you a strong enough push to get there. You need to know exactly what achieving this goal will do for you. Remember: your 'whys' need to be bigger than the hurdles you may face, otherwise you will not overcome them.

What are you prepared to give up? – Everyone is happy to talk about what they want but no one likes to think about what they have to give up to get there. Everything you want you can get if you want it badly enough, as long as you are prepared to sacrifice to achieve your goals. Remember: the biggest rewards come from the greatest sacrifices.

Affirmations – The way you talk to yourself and what you say to yourself are powerful tools on the path to achieving your goals. Negative self-talk will only lead to pessimism and you will continue to fall short of achieving your goals. Specific positive language will guide you to the correct way to affirm who you are, and will influence your personality and attitude, aiding you on your journey to success. Remember: it is extremely important to ensure the affirmations you state are linked closely to your goals.

Visualisation – Involve your senses. The aim here is to engage your body with your goal setting alongside your mind. Be in the present: make your goals feel as if they are being achieved right now or have already been achieved. Remember: get as many of your senses involved as possible.

Reflection – the Vital Bonus Step – Reflection is key. It is amazing how motivating it can be to see how far you have come on your way to achieving your goals. If you feel as if you are far away from them, you can reflect on what you have done in the past to get to where you are now. It also is a driving force in setting new goals as you can reflect on the previous goals you have already achieved and can see what to do differently when moving forward. Remember: the only time we look back is to see how far we have come.

The Side Effect – Tying your goals together to ensure a deeper meaning can increase your motivation and reduce the chances of an anti-climax. Remember: You have the ability to make the goal mean something bigger than the goal itself.

Upgrading Your Mindset – Shift your focus towards making yourself a valuable asset. As you invest more time and energy over the years this asset will become more valuable. Remember: Be patient with the macro but aggressive with the micro.

Evolving goals and rebalancing

Most people get discouraged if they set a goal and do not achieve it on the exact date they desire. Although I agree that you should work towards the date as closely as possible, it is also extremely important to acknowledge that when you are taken off track you must rebalance yourself and keep moving forward. Take comfort in knowing that people have achieved some of the greatest goals after countless setbacks. Sometimes your goals may even evolve. Be prepared and open-minded in this regard, as sometimes your goals can grow into something bigger than what was initially anticipated. Having a goal that is inflexible could lead to you giving up. By understanding these principles, you will remain positive throughout your journey.

You now have all the steps you need to keep yourself focused and on the path to achieving your goals. You have learnt about how positive self-talk can influence your ability to achieve your goals and how you need to interlink your goals into most areas of your life. Fed up with your job and want to set up a business? Remember, the wages you are earning can help you to build the capital you need. The values you hold will impact on the goals that are most important to you and you will therefore be more likely to achieve them more quickly.

Whether you have monetary, entrepreneurial, physical, spiritual or any other kind of goals, these steps can guide you on your way to achieving any goal you set your mind to.

> *The Side Effect of following the principles in this book is that you will live a more intentional life with the ability to be, do and have anything you desire in life.*

'The greatest danger for most of us is not that our aim is too high and we miss it but that it is too low and we reach it.'

—Michelangelo

Thank you for taking the time to read this book. I hope you take away as much as possible that is of value and use it to project you towards achieving any goal you set your mind to. I am a strong believer in a person's ability to accomplish anything that they really want to, and that we are all geniuses, destined for greatness, but sometimes we just need a little guidance to unlock our full potential.

'Allow your passion to become your purpose, and it will someday become your profession.'

—*Gabrielle Bernstein*

ABOUT THE AUTHOR

Mark is an entrepreneur, investor and foreign exchange trader from the UK. His early years in the world of work were not as successful as he had initially hoped. He began training as an engineer at the age of 17 but was made redundant as the firm collapsed in the midst of the 2008 financial crisis. He then adjusted his perspective on his future, initially working for a very short time as a labourer before switching to build himself up to working in a position as a broker in the City. Coming from a working-class family, Mark has always striven for more in order to provide for his family and to build a better life for them all.

He is now the owner of multiple businesses in areas including software development, personal development and foreign exchange trading education, teaching novice through to experienced traders. He began trading forex at the age of 18 whilst working in his various positions and now trades fulltime whilst running his companies. Falcon FX Ltd was his way of teaching others the skills he himself had learnt. Passing on the unique style of trading he has since developed, he wanted to help others to do what he has, to leave the nine to five of employment and become fulltime forex traders, to have the flexibility and freedom to live the lives they dream of.

Mark found personal development around the same time he was introduced to forex trading and is passionate about developing his mind, as well as his body. He strongly believes in becoming the best version of himself through continued learning. Goal setting became a great passion of his. He quickly learnt that by writing down his goals and adjusting and developing his formula, he could keep himself focused and continue to work towards his goals in a state of flow. Continually refining his goal setting formula, he came to the realisation that it could help others become more intentional and not just himself. After firstly sharing it with those close to him and seeing how powerfully the changes were that occurred, he was compelled to share what he had learnt and developed with others, empowering them to aim towards achieving their goals so that they too could benefit from this formula.

EXAMPLE GOAL

Shaun:

Goal Date: 31 December 2021

Detail:

On or before 31 December 2021, I am 10% body fat and very physically fit. I am lean and muscular. I have broad, round and muscular shoulders, and toned and strong arms. My chest is defined and I have a visible six-pack. I have a noticeable 'sweep' of my quads, defined hamstring muscles and lifted glutes. My calves are strong and toned. I have a 32-inch waist and a 40-inch chest. I weigh 80 kilograms, which is ideal for my height of 6ft. I can run a five-minute mile. I have the athletic build of a swimmer.

Manageable Steps:

1. I have set myself four months to lose 8kg of fat at a rate of 2kg per month and build myself a leaner, stronger, more muscular physique.
2. I go to the gym five times a week, training each muscle group as follows:

   Monday - Back and biceps
   Tuesday - Legs (quad and calves) and abdominals
   Wednesday – Shoulders

Thursday - Chest and triceps
Friday - Legs (hamstring) and abdominals

3. I do cardio training three times a week at the end of my session for thirty minutes, one day of low intensity steady state (LISS) training, one day of high intensity interval training (HIIT) and one day of swimming. This is to ensure I am burning fat as well as maintaining muscle.

Monday - HIIT
Wednesday - LISS
Thursday – Swimming

4. On a Sunday, one of my days off from the gym, I go for a five-kilometre run.
5. I have a macro-controlled meal plan that ensures I consume exactly what I need daily to push me closer to achieving my target physique. Within this I take protein powder in my shake straight after the gym to help repair my muscles, as well as fish-oil tablets once a day for my joints and bones and BCAAs during my session to prevent lean muscle mass loss. I plan my meals on a Sunday evening and prepare Monday's and Tuesday's food on a Sunday evening, Wednesday's and Thursday's food on a Tuesday evening, and Friday's, Saturday's and Sunday's food on a Thursday evening.
6. On a Saturday evening I allow myself one 'treat' meal where I have any dinner and dessert I wish. This satisfies my craving for foods I know I shouldn't have and therefore keeps me focused throughout the week.
7. I drink three litres of Ph 9.5 Alkaline water every day as I am aware how important it is to keep my body hydrated, especially when training.
8. I take weekly progress pictures on a Sunday and compare them monthly to review my progress.
9. I am aware there may be interruptions to my gym plan, and that I may not always be able to stick completely to

my gym days. However, I know there is flexibility in the days I can train as I can always make up missed sessions on Saturdays and Sundays.

Skills and Knowledge required:

1. I am having one session a week with a personal trainer who is teaching me how to remain focused and keeping me on track with my food and progress, as well as pushing me in the intense gym sessions and teaching me the correct method for different exercises. This is something extra to hold me accountable, as I know he will be checking up on my measurements, weight, how much weight I can push/pull and how my fitness is progressing.
2. I am seeking continual advice from a nutritionist to ensure my macro-controlled meal plan keeps my body fuelled properly and is as healthy as possible.

Obstacles:

1. Fast food - I am focusing on my macro-controlled meal plan and living a healthy, sustainable lifestyle.
2. Alcohol - I am aware of the benefits of keeping my body hydrated and therefore I am focusing on the benefits of water on my physiology.
3. Social gatherings - Most restaurants cater for a healthy lifestyle, and therefore when I go out to eat with my friends, I ensure I stick to the usual foods I would eat within my meal plan so as not to undo any hard work I have put in.

People to associate with:

1. Hardworking, driven individuals such as my colleagues at work
2. Darren, my gym partner, who is on the same fitness journey
3. My personal trainer, who is a fitness enthusiast
4. People striving to achieve goals in general and likeminded people who share similar values

What's in it for me and why?

I achieve this goal to have a happy, healthy and long life. What's in it for me is a sustainable lifestyle where I feel great about myself, have a healthy body, clothes that fit better and feel a sense of achievement. Every time I weigh myself and am closer to my target weight I feel proud; every time I am able to lift more weight or do more repetitions of an exercise I know I have achieved something.

What am I prepared to give up?

I am prepared to give up foods that do not fit into my meal plan, alcohol as it will not be beneficial to my progress, nights out that may tempt me to cheat on my plan, and Friday night movie nights as I am now training in the gym on Friday evenings. I am prepared to give up free/leisure time in order to visit my personal trainer and nutritionist, go to the gym and prepare and plan my food for the coming week. I will still have time to see my friends/family/partner but I am prepared to give up the appropriate amount of my free/leisure time necessary to achieve this goal.

Affirmations:

I am 10% body fat on or before 31 December 2021.
I am 10% body fat on or before 31 December 2021.
I am 10% body fat on or before 31 December 2021.
I am 10% body fat on or before 31 December 2021.
I am 10% body fat on or before 31 December 2021.

I live a healthy lifestyle.
I live a healthy lifestyle.
I live a healthy lifestyle.
I live a healthy lifestyle.
I live a healthy lifestyle.

I am strong, lean, toned and feel in great shape.
I am strong, lean, toned and feel in great shape.
I am strong, lean, toned and feel in great shape.

I am strong, lean, toned and feel in great shape.
I am strong, lean, toned and feel in great shape.

I always look forward to my workout.
I always look forward to my workout.
I always look forward to my workout.
I always look forward to my workout.
I always look forward to my workout.

I train hard, with intensity in every session.
I train hard, with intensity in every session.
I train hard, with intensity in every session.
I train hard, with intensity in every session.
I train hard, with intensity in every session.

Visualisation:

I am 10% body fat. I see that my clothes fit exactly how I want them to. I feel comfortable and confident. I can see that I have a lean and athletic shape in the mirror and feel great within myself. I see that I look better and hear people pay me regular compliments. I feel positive that I have achieved a lean body that I continually sustain.

Not only is my body lean and athletic looking, my face is more chiselled and slimmer and my cheekbones are now more prominent. When running I feel healthy, fast and agile. My friends/family/partner/colleagues look up to me as they see me as a person who is disciplined in achieving goals and can see the progress I have made.

I am on holiday in Mexico. I am lean and in my swim shorts walking towards the sea. I can hear the sounds of the sea, smell salt water, taste the fresh orange juice I have just left beside my sun lounger, feel the sand beneath my feet and sun on my back, and can look down and see my visible abdominals, muscular legs and lean physique. I feel incredible within myself knowing that I am in great shape, knowing that I have achieved my goal of a lean physique by committing to my plans and staying focused. I feel confident in myself and I can achieve any goal I put my mind to with the right steps.

Reflection:

I reflect on my goal every month to see how far I have come.

ONE MONTH LATER…

Reflection:

I am one month into my fitness journey. I have lost 2kg, an inch from my waist and am lifting significantly more weight than I was before. I have cut thirty seconds from my minutes per mile and can already run for longer than before. I am feeling super motivated as I am right on track. I am 25% towards achieving my goal with three months to go. Being on a calorie deficit has made me feel slightly fatigued, but I have been pushing through by keeping my goal at the forefront of my thoughts. Seeing the results has pushed me further forward and kept me disciplined. I will keep my focus and look forward to checking again in a month's time to monitor my improved progress.

GOALS WORKSHEETS

Below are a number of worksheets that can be printed in order to complete the main exercises presented in this book. I usually write my goals in full in a journal but everyone works differently. If you are better off with worksheets, then the following pages will be helpful for you.

10 Things I Want to Be, Do and Have:

Be

1. _____

2. _____

3. _____

4. _____

5. _____

6. _____

7. _____

8. _____

9. _____

10. _____

Do

1. _____

2. _____

3. _____

4. _____

5. _____

6. _____

7. _____

8. _____

9. _____

10. _____

THE SIDE EFFECT

<u>Have</u>

1. _____

2. _____

3. _____

4. _____

5. _____

6. _____

7. _____

8. _____

9. _____

10. _____

Set a date:

Goal: _____

_____

_____

Deadline: _____

Potential Constraints:

1. _____

_____

2. _____

_____

3. _____

_____

4. _____

_____

5. _____

_____

Detail is key:

Date:_____

Goal_____

_____

_____

_____

_____

_____

_____

_____

_____

_____

_____

_____

_____

_____

_____

_____

Signature:_____

Manageable steps:

Goal: _____

_____

Manageable steps:

1._____

_____

2._____

_____

3._____

_____

4. _____

_____

5._____

_____

6._____

_____

7. _____

_____

8. _____

_____

Possible Mentors:

1. _____ 2. _____

3. _____ 4. _____

Knowledge questions to ask:

1. _____

_____

2. _____

_____

3. _____

_____

4. _____

_____

Skills questions to ask:

1. _____

_____

2. _____

_____

3. _____

_____

4. _____

_____

Knowledge and Skills:

1. _____

_____

_____

_____

2. _____

_____

_____

_____

3. _____

_____

_____

_____

4. _____

_____

_____

_____

5. _____

_____

_____

_____

6. _____

_____

_____

_____

7. _____

_____

_____

_____

8. _____

_____

_____

_____

9. _____

_____

_____

_____

Identify your obstacles:

1. Hurdle_____

Solution_____

2. Hurdle_____

Solution_____

3. Hurdle_____

Solution_____

4. Hurdle_____

Solution_____

5. Hurdle_____

Solution_____

6. Hurdle_____

Solution_____

7. Hurdle_____

Solution_____

People to associate with:

Person _____

Red Flags: Green Flags:

_____   _____

_____   _____

_____   _____

_____   _____

_____   _____

_____   _____

_____   _____

_____   _____

_____   _____

_____   _____

_____   _____

_____   _____

_____   _____

_____   _____

_____   _____

_____   _____

_____   _____

<u>What is in it for you and why?</u>

Why do I want to achieve this goal?

1. _____

_____

2. _____

_____

3. _____

_____

4. _____

_____

5. _____

_____

6. _____

_____

7. _____

_____

8. _____

_____

9 _____

_____

10. _____

_____

<u>What is in it for me?</u>

1. _____

_____

2. _____

_____

3. _____

_____

4. _____

_____

5. _____

_____

6. _____

_____

7. _____

_____

8. _____

_____

9. _____

_____

10. _____

_____

How I spend my time now (fill in blanks with other time-consuming activities):

	M	T	W	T	F	S	S	Total
Work								
Travel								
Sleeping								
Food/Food Prep								
Showering/Dressing								
Out (Friends)								
Out (Partner)								
Family Time								
TV								
Housework								

How I want to/will now spend my time (fill in blanks with other time-consuming activities):

	M	T	W	T	F	S	S	Total
Work								
Travel								
Sleeping								
Food/Food Prep								
Showering/Dressing								
Out (Friends)								
Out (Partner)								
Family Time								
TV								
Housework								

Affirmations:

Take one of your goals and think of two specific and relevant affirmations that apply. Write them out in the correct format and language, keeping them positive and located in the present.

Goal:

_____

Affirmation 1:

1._____

2._____

3._____

4._____

5._____

6._____

7._____

8._____

9._____

10._____

Affirmation 2:

1._____

2._____

3._____

4._____

5._____

6._____

7._____

8._____

9._____

10._____

Affirmation 3:

1._____

2._____

3._____

4._____

5._____

6._____

7._____

8._____

9._____

10._____

Visualisation:

Consider your five senses: sight, touch, taste, sound and smell. Pick four of them (I understand that taste can be difficult to apply to many goals) and choose four ways in which you will engage your senses to better visualise your goal.

Goal:

_____

_____

Sense 1: _____

_____

_____

Sense 2: _____

_____

_____

Sense 3: _____

_____

_____

Sense 4: _____

_____

_____

Reflection:

Goal: _____

_____

Question: What have I done since my last reflection that has pushed me closer to achieving my goal?

1. _____

_____

2. _____

_____

3. _____

_____

4. _____

_____

Question: Have I encountered any hurdles since my last reflection? If so, what were they?

1. _____

_____

2. _____

_____

3. _____

_____

4. _____

_____

Question: How did I overcome this hurdle?

1. _____

_____

2. _____

_____

3. _____

_____

4. _____

_____

Question: How much closer am I to my goal?

_____

_____

_____

_____

_____

_____

Question: What can I do this month that will push me further in the right direction?

1. _____

_____

2. _____

_____

3. _____

_____

4. _____

_____

Date:_____

Daily Goals:

1._____

2._____

3._____

4._____

5._____

Daily Values:

1._____

2._____

3._____

4._____

5._____

Affirmations:

Affirmation 1:

_____

_____

Affirmation 2:

_____

_____

Affirmation 3:

_____

_____

Affirmation 4:

_____

_____

Affirmation 5:

_____

_____

Bonus exercise:

To ensure that your goals are fully aligned with your values, you can use this sheet.

Daily Goals:

1._____

2._____

3._____

4._____

5._____

Daily Values:

1._____

2._____

3._____

4._____

5._____

Link – here you should write the reasons why your values and goals are aligned.

Goal _____ links to Value _____ because_____

_____

Goal _____ links to Value _____ because_____

_____

Goal _____ links to Value _____ because_____

_____

Goal _____ links to Value _____ because_____

_____

Goal _____ links to Value _____ because_____

_____

Goal _____ links to Value _____ because_____

_____

Goal _____ links to Value _____ because_____

_____

THE SIDE EFFECT

Goal _____ links to Value _____ because_____

_____

Goal _____ links to Value _____ because_____

_____

Goal _____ links to Value _____ because_____

_____

Goal _____ links to Value _____ because_____

_____

Goal _____ links to Value _____ because_____

_____

Goal _____ links to Value _____ because_____

_____

THE STORY OF THE FALCON AND THE CROW

As the Falcon was out flying one day with his friend the Crow, he took the opportunity to look around and marvel at the world. Whilst looking up, he spotted a Falcon that was flying at a speed and height greater than he himself had ever attempted.

The Crow turned to the Falcon and said "Why are you looking up there? That's way too high, we can't go there," and carried on flying.

The Falcon calls out to the other Falcon to slow down and fly slower so he can speak to him but receives no response. Frustrated by the other bird, he pushes himself to fly higher and faster, gaining the same pace as the Falcon that was previously above him and leaving his friend below shocked.

This other Falcon was older, larger, stronger and faster than he. In an attempt to catch up with him he tried to fly faster. The young Falcon began to fly faster than he ever had before and called out to his fellow Falcon "How is it that you fly so fast? I am like you but I am struggling to keep up with your speed?"

"Patience, perseverance and practice" replied the older Falcon, "Remember you're a Falcon not a Crow" before flying higher and out of sight.

Crows can only fly at the heights of tall trees but Falcons can fly thousands of feet in the air. In life, you are going to be surrounded by both Falcons and Crows. Sometimes your goals and ambitions are going to be so big that they seem unobtainable to some people but easily achievable to others. The Crows will be those people with limiting beliefs, who think and feel they can only go so far, and only fly so high in life. The Falcons are those who let nothing and no one stand in their way, and who believe they are capable of anything with the right focus and determination. Falcons are fast, accurate and precise and can see their prey (goal) far in the distance when a Crow cannot.

Now and again, a Crow will look up and see a Falcon flying above them and feel uncomfortable. They will try to bring the Falcon down to their level. The Falcon can adapt and fly lower, at the height of the Crow. The Crow, however, can never fly at the height of a Falcon.

Printed in Great Britain
by Amazon

59911287R00111